पुरातत्व
पुरातत्त्व
PURĀTATTVA

Bulletin of the Indian Archaeological Society

No. 4 1970-71

V.D. Krishnaswami Commemoration Volume

Editor
S.P. Gupta

Assistant Editors
P.C. Pant
K.N. Dikshit
B.M. Pande

D.K. Printworld (P) Ltd.
New Delhi

Cataloging in Publication Data — DK
[Courtesy : D.K. Agencies (P) Ltd. <docinfo@dkagencies.com>]

Purātattva : bulletin of the Indian Archaeological Society, no. 4, 1970-71 : V.D. Krishnaswami commemoration volume / editor, S.P. Gupta ; assistant editors, P.C. Pant, K.N. Dikshit, B.M. Pande.

p. cm.
Includes bibliographical references.
ISBN 8124602808

1. Archaeology — India — Periodicals. 2. India — Antiquities — Periodicals. 3. India — Civilization — Periodicals. I. Krishnaswami, V.D. II. Gupta, S.P. III. Indian Archaeological Society.

First Reprinted in 2005
ISBN 81-246-0280-8
Price for volume 4 (1970-71): Rs. 600 US $ 30

Reprint authorised by
Indian Archaeological Society
New Delhi - 110 016

Purātattva is published annually.
Manuscripts (whether in the form of articles or notes or book reviews) offered for publication should be sent to the Editor, Purātattva, Indian Archaeological Society, B-17, Qutab Institutional Area, New Delhi - 110 016.

Published and printed by:
D.K. Printworld (P) Ltd.
'Srikunj,' F-52, Bali Nagar
New Delhi – 110015
Phone : (011) 2545 3975, 2546 6019 Fax : (011) 2546 5926
E-mail : dkprintworld@vsnl.net
www. dkprintworld.com

CONTENTS

Editorial

The Indian Archaeological Society was formed at Varanasi in 1967 largely due to the personal efforts of Prof. A. K. Narain of the Banaras Hindu University, who was also its General Secretary till 1970, and Prof. H. D. Sankalia of the Deccan College, Poona, who has been its Chairman ever since. From the very beginning its heavy load of day-to-day work was borne by its young and energetic Asstt. Secretary Shri O. P. Tandon (now Deputy Registrar, B.H.U.). At one stage it appeared that the Society may remain confined to the non-governmental people since Shri A. Ghosh, the then Director General of Archaeology, had some sharp differences over the constitution of the Society. I very well recollect that meeting of the Executive Committee at Varanasi in which Prof. Narain expressed his great concern over the dispute. Rai Govind Chandra, the then treasurer, was very critical of the Archaeological Survey's attitude towards the Society. Luckily amogst us was Prof. S. Nurul Hasan, (now Minister of State for Education and Social Welfare) as one of our Vice-Presidents. As the passions rose very high he quietly came to the dias and one by one proposed such commendable amendments which were readily acceptable to all present there, including myself who represented one of the Governmental institutions. On my return to Delhi I reported the whole thing to Shri Ghosh who was naturally very happy to learn the suitable amendments. Needless to say, since then the Society really became the first non-governmental professional body of archaeologists working in any capacity within the Govt. or outside. We are now a group of more than a hundred workers from all over the country.

From the very beginning the Society started publishing its own Bulletin called 'Puratattva', the Sanskrit word for 'archaeology'. Till 1970 it had already brought out three numbers. The entire credit for their publication goes to Prof. Narain since he managed it without any financial support from anywhere. Then, in Nov. 1970 the Annual Conference was held at Nagpur in which Prof. Narain proposed to Shri B.K. Thapar to become the General Secretary of the Society since he was shortly leaving for the U.S.A. as a visiting professor. Consequent upon this, Shri K.N. Dikshit, was elected its Asstt. Secretary and Treasurer, and I was given the editorship of the Bulletin. As luck would have it, Shri Thapar left for Cambridge in early 1971 and Shri Dikshit had to carry out the entire work of the Society, which I must say, he did very well. In May 1971 he even organized a Seminar on OCP and NBP Ware, the proceedings of which is now through the press. As far as I am concerned, the Bulletin is with you which records my failings more than success.

★

One thing for which we heartily thank the Director General of the Archaeological Survey of India and the Ministry of Education & Social Welfare is the grant of

Rs. 3,000/- for the publication of two issues of our Bulletin—nos. 4 & 5. Although, it is a very meager amount considering our nature of publications, still a happy beginning has been made and we hope that the Govt. will be helping the Society in the future also with a bigger amount so that we may publish regularly, two numbers of the Bulletin, and Proceedings of the seminars that the Society holds annually.

★

I take this occassion to report with great sorrow the sudden demise of V. D. Krishnaswami at Hyderabad, Andhra Pradesh, at the age of 64. His life had somewhat of a fictional quality abut it, but his work was well-grounded in reality. His field research ranged from the palaeolithic camps in the foot-hills of the Himalayas to the Iron Age megalithic cemeteries in Kerala. To each one he brought those talents which were peculiarly his. He was always a very demanding man, of himself and of those who worked with him. By nature he was an extremely jolly man but he had also that infinite patience for detail which provided real substance and validity to the results of his researches. Acute observation in the field, an all-inclusiveness in recording and a search for proper terminology in the context of Indian prehistory were second nature of 'V.D.K.'—as we used to call him fondly.

He started his career as an extremely rash young student and ended with a very worldly-wise man. He often used to repeat two dictums of his life: firstly, Make others Great, they will make you Greater ! and secondly, in order to run an institution Man is more important than his knowledge.

We dedicate this number of the Bulletin to his memory as a tribute to his humane nature, erudite scholarship and rare organizational ability.

★

The present number of the Bulletin includes the report by Shri B. B. Lal of the outstanding discovery by him and Shri B. K. Thapar in the entire history of archaeological researches in the world—the remains of a ploughed field at Kalibangan, going back to 2300 B.C. or more.

Dr. B. S. Verma, presently in the Archaeological Survey of India, Patna, reports the neolithic complex of his excavations at Chirand. The complex is marked by a large number of bone and antler tools of a variety not found so far anywhere in India. Significantly enough, it also includes pots with tubular and channel spouts as well as Burnished Grey Ware with post-firing red ochre painting, analogous to those found in the Neolithic-Chalcolithic context of Western India. On the basis of C^{14} dates the earliest date of this complex goes back to 1900 B.C. The discovery, therefore, leads us to revise some of our tacitly accepted views on the Neolithic-Chalcolithic cultures given during the last two decades by Prof. H. D. Sankalia and Dr. F. R. Allchin. Their theory of Iranian origin of these features may now be reopened for discussions.

The article by Dr. M. K. Dhavalikar of the Deccan College, Poona, takes into account the results of his recent excavations of Chalcolithic Kayatha. Herein he reviews their implications on the colonization of Malwa by the Kayatha folk. He also discusses the character, origin and development of the chalcolithic cultures in that region. He particularly deals with a very important aspect of this culture, viz. the Cult of the Bull. He, like Dr. B. S. Verma, also pleads for the revision of the existing views on the origin of the channel spouted bowl in Malwa. According to him they are likely to be indigenous and not Iranian.

Dr. F. Khan is our leading Palaeontologist. He has, in his paper, worked out a revised scheme of Pleistocene events in India on the basis of his studies on the mammalian fauna. Thus, to the utter dismay of many of us, he says that 'the mammalian fauna existing in India from the first to the third glaciation is unknown so far, and......the fauna of the last glacial age is scantily recognized'. Unfortunately, in the present study he has not taken into account the fossils which have been collected by Prof. Sankalia in a closely observed stratigraphy at Nevasa, etc., or Prof. G.R. Sharma's collections from the regular deposits of the River Belan in U.P.

Shri R. C. Gaur of the University of Aligarh in his masterly analysis of the proto-historic problems of the Ganga-Yamuna doab has tried to work out the cross-currents of the cultures from the Pre-Harappan times to the beginning of the Iron Age. He has specially dealt with the problem of the OCP and his excavations at Lal Qila.

My own paper is an attempt to find out the answer of one of the age old problems with us—what was the immediate source of the Indian megaliths? There seems to be some good evidence which indicates the Gulf of Oman as the probable source but more field work in south-east Arabia alone can give it the required exactness.

★

In this number we have added a few new columns: 'Notes and News' and 'Readings in Indian Archaeology'. Both the columns are designed to make the journal most useful to the research workers, particularly in India. The 'Notes and News' contains short articles on new discoveries focussing our attention pointedly to one problem at a time as also the programmes of forthcoming seminars, lectures, etc., to be organized by learned Societies and Institutions. The 'Readings in Indian Archaeology' contains the clippings from important articles published in those foreign journals which are normally not available in Indian Universities.

S. P. Gupta

V.D. Krishnaswami (18-01-1905/15-07-1970)

V. D. Krishnaswami (18-1-1905/15-7-1970)

The otherwise complacent cockles of official Indian archaeology received a flutter of fraternal anguish at the most unexpected passing away at Bangalore on 15th July 1970 of V. D. Kirshnaswami, M. A., Dip. Arch. (Cantab)., during a post-operative convalescence which did not hold out any major threat to his life. It might be conventional to say that a leading Prehistorian and field expert in India had been snatched away from our midst. But it would be no platitude to add that with his passing away, a transition from one age to another had been heralded. Anyone who had even had a nodding acquaintance with the outwardly forbidding but inwardly genial personality of Krishnaswami would have to carry the memories for a life time. In fact, the entry by Krishnaswami into any company, social or academic, immediately electrified the atmosphere for, in the style of his performance, he was often not unlike the mastodens stampeding across primeval swamps.

Born in a Tamil Vaisnavaite family in a village which had produced legal luminaries and public figures, when Krishnaswami qualified himself for a geologist's profession by graduating from the Madras University, and immediately started casting a good look at the Pleistocene environment of early man around Madras for launching on its study, it could almost have been the unexpressed dream-desire of Bruce Foote fulfilled, in this part of our land. But the agonising pilgrimage he made from stage of acquisition of firm knowledge and the tools for his job, to the attainment of necessary opportunity and the station for getting recognition therefrom had been, in his case, a vital factor which moulded his temperament and produced an aggressive and restless personality. Undeterred by set-backs or administrative vicissitudes, he had always kept his goals clear in any venture, and had brought to their achievement a spectacular, and provocatively novel and positive character.

His collaboration in the Yale-Cambridge Expeditions of 1935 for the Himalayan Glacial studies in Kashmir under Dr. Helmut De Terra and later, his intensive continuation of work with Paterson in the area around Madras where he had started his pioneering studies of Early Man, a few years before, are all part of his unflagging zeal in the work. His early academic laurels were reflected in his stint as a teacher of geology and geography, and in his becoming recipient of a fellowship of the University of Madras that enabled him to repair to the University of Cambridge where he acquired the Diploma in Archaeology and worked under Prof. Miles Burkitt, and fully utilised the opportunity for extensively familiarising himself with Stone Age studies in France, Germany, etc., in the company of such acknowledged stalwarts as Abbe Breuil, Vallois, Peyrony and Frederick Zeuner.

These were followed up with his share in India subsequently in the Gujarat Prehistoric Expedition 1940 along with Dr. Sankalia, and later his organising the Pan Indian Prehistoric Expedition with Dr. Zeuner in 1950. Those who were associated with him in the field have realised how much of an insight he had in field studies especially in original physiomorphic and typological aspects of Stone Age research. His other great work was the first organised exploration and scientific documentation of the megalithic monuments and types in Chingleput, Pudukkottai and Cochin between 1944-50 which he completed for the Archaeological Survey of India with his characteristic meticulousness, not only resulting in many technical papers by him and jointly with his colleagues in the meanwhile for the Science Congress and other learned bodies, but also the opening up of the entire megalithic problem, thanks to a working standardisation of nomenclature for this study.

Lest we should anticipate his later career too soon, it should be recorded that Krishnaswami was the first official Prehistorian of the Government of India, consequent on the specific recommendation in his Report by Sir Leonard Wolley, the celebrated Sumerian Archaeologist, for promotion of prehistoric studies by the Archaeological Survey of India in 1944, and the assumption of the office of the Director General of Archaeology in India, by Dr. (now Sir) R. E. M. Wheeler, for initiation of the reorganisation of the field programmes of the Survey. Working from Madras, it was then that the Stone Age and Megalithic studies were popularised by Krishnaswami and resulted in such comprehensive papers by him as 'Stone Age India' published in *Ancient India,* No. 3. His later enlargement of the megalithic studies in south India, as narrated earlier, were found summarised in his paper on the 'Megalithic types of India' published in *Ancient India*, No. 5. His sectional Presidential address to the Indian Science Congress meet at Delhi in 1958 on the 'Neolithic Pattern in India' stands out the most provocative and immaculate presentation of a difficult thesis, with a rare synthesisation of regional milieu.

In the Archaeological Survey of India, where he held successively the posts of Superintendent in various Circles and Dy. Director General (Explorations), he had organised and assisted in many field projects and trained a host of young scholars. The Fort Museum at Madras is a testimony to his powers of organisation and action, at the opportune moment. On his retirement from the Survey, he was invited by the authorities of the Indian Museum, Calcutta, to function as its Director, and later he held the Directorship of Salar Jung National Museum, Hyderabad. At the very time of his sudden demise, he was slated for the Directorship of another important Science and Art Museum at Hyderabad.

A man with a perennial fund of a somewhat wry humour and an infectious gusto, liable to be occasionally interrupted by wild outbursts that left him remorseful only too soon, his was a colourful personality by any standards. Through his original and pioneering early field research in the prehistory of south India, he had most deservedly written himself into the annals of these studies, as one of its esteemed savants.

In a commemorative context such as the present one, it would be pardonable to present the foibles as well as the flairs of the person under study and no colourful figure was ever without being controversial either, and 'V. D. K.'—as he was familiarly abbreviated by all his Indian colleagues—had these traits in abundant measure. There was an aura of a permanent campaigner about him, and while he did not collect any court around him as some of the less well endowed bureaucrats are apt to, he did keep a crack personal squad for launching invisible action, when called for, and certainly in scouting talent of miscellaneous kinds for all contingencies, minor or major, among his friends, colleagues and subordinates, he was unrivalled. It was indeed fascinating to watch him in the midst of his performance. He always plumped for the strategic rather than the tactical, and kept his machinery well oiled. His roving eye always unerringly caught, whether in an advertisement of merchandise or in a research paper, the data that is most striking and useful, and he made careful note of these for further utilisation by him or his colleagues. His tours were marathon affairs—typical of his age—with the commissariat given extra attention; for, though personally he was far from being a gourmet, he was nevertheless, a discerning gastronomist, and one who dispensed the day with one square meal when necessary, but with unspecified rounds of snacks, where available.

There were many apocryphal stories about him, some of which he himself narrated with gusto, for he had a knack of turning even permanent enemies into temporary friends. At the behest of Wheeler, at Brahmagiri he once literally jumped into the trench to show his alertness and all but broke his ankle. He was a window-dresser *par excellence* and one who kept his humour intact, even when his luck and status were at the lowest ebb, so that when the brighter day dawned, he could remain unscathed. His own personality underwent psychosomatic changes, with the passing years, and even his close colleagues were sometimes flabbergasted by his atrocious changes of apparel, including a long saffron robe, wooden sandals and a swirling walking stick, and he had once well nigh dismayed and confounded some of his own close kinfolk, by masquerading in false moustaches and beard and being close at hand but undiscovered at an airport on arrival.

While, his acumen and wordly wisdom of an unabashed kind made him a picturesque colleague, his keen analytical powers had also led him into the realms of the occult and clairvoyance and, as a matter of fact, he was an intuitive palmist who delved with assiduity into the available literature and empirical palmistry studies.

Tagore had said that 'without making the pilgrimage, you cannot reach the shrine'. V. D. K. did make his ardent and arduous pilgrimage. Could he reach the shrine ? Only the Almighty, in whose bosom he now rests, would know the answer.

—K. V. Soundara Rajan

PERHAPS THE EARLIEST PLOUGHED FIELD SO FAR EXCAVATED ANYWHERE IN THE WORLD

B. B. LAL

The Archaeological Survey of India, under the joint direction of the present writer and his colleague, Shri B. K. Thapar, has just completed its excavations at Kalibangan in District Ganganagar, Rajasthan, a site now well known for the remains of the Indus Civilization.

Situated on the left bank of the Ghaggar river, which has dried up since the ancient times, the Indus settlement is divisible into two parts which, following the pattern of Harappa and Mohenjo-daro, comprise a 'citadel' on the west and a 'lower town' on the east.

However, what is more important about the excavations at Kalibangan is the discovery of a settlement which even preceded that of the Indus Civilization (also known as the Harappa Culture, after the name of the place where it was first identified). Thus, below the Harappan 'citadel' have been found the remains of a small township which represents a culture different from the mature Harappa Culture, yet which may have contributed to the make-up of the latter in some ways. This pre-Harappan township was itself fortified and, indeed, as the excavations revealed, the Harappans utilized the pre-Harrappan town-wall by incorporating its northern and western sides into their own citadel-wall.

These pre-Harappan people enjoyed a fairly advanced material culture though, no doubt, it was not so much advanced as the Harappa Culture itself. They lived in well-planned mud-brick houses as did their successors, used well-fired red pottery, often slipped and painted with nice geometric floral and faunal designs, had overground as well as underground ovens (resembling the modern *tandurs*) for cooking, domesticated the cattle, carried on agriculture and used, besides blades and arrowheads of chalcedony, jasper, etc., copper implements to meet their every-day needs. Amongst the major items that stand out in contrast between the equipment of the pre-Harappan and the Harappan people are seals and sealings and weights and measures, used by the latter. One does not know as to what impelled human beings, to originate writing, but if it be commerce and trade, as is not unlikely, the pre-Harappan people of Kalibangan perhaps had yet to grow their wings.

Be that as it may. The pre-Harappans of Kalibangan have given us a unique example of a ploughed field. To the south-east of their settlement, well away from their town-wall, have been discovered the remains of an agricultural field having furrow-marks on a grid pattern (plates I and II). The two sets of marks run at right angles to each other and approximately north-south and east-west respectively. The average distance between the individual furrows of the former set is 1·90 metres, while in the latter case it is 30 centimetres. It was also observed that the north-south furrows with greater intermediary spacing overran the east-west ones with shorter spacing (cf. plates I and II). This shows that the short-space ones were ploughed first, and then the ones having greater spacing in between.

As these marks began to appear on the ground during the course of excavation, discussions as to their probable purpose also commenced. Thus, when at the initial stage only a few short-space lines were observed it was thought that these might represent the impressions of some wooden construction which fell on the ground and got decomposed, although it was also felt that these might be furrows of an ancient field. Within a few days came to be exposed the lines running at right angles to the former. The wood-impression interpretation began to lose ground, although it was still argued by a few that the cross-lines might represent cross-bars used in the construction. In the course of time when a sizable area (about 4×4 m.) of these grid-pattern lines was exposed, the wood-structure theory began to recede to the background, and the furrow-theory gained ground. (Finally, the furrow-marks were traced in an area measuring about 14×10 metres.) However, it was difficult to explain fully the grid-pattern of the furrows. A survey of the fields around Kalibangan was then undertaken, and it was a most pleasant surprise to find that amongst the various patterns followed in the region was also one which tallied with that excavated. It even agreed in certain essential details. Thus, on plate III may be seen a modern field which shows not merely a grid-pattern of furrows but also that in one set the intermediary space between the furrows is much greater than in the other. Also, the superimposition of the furrows shows that the set with greater spacing has been ploughed later than the other one. This is exactly what had happened in the case of the excavated field.

While the similarity of the ploughing pattern confirmed the idea that the excavated lines represented an ancient field, the question that still remaind to be answered was: why such a pattern ? Further enquiries were made which revealed that this pattern was adopted to accommodate two kinds of crops in one field. Later on, it was observed that in the furrows with short intermediary

Plate I. Kalibangan, Pre-Harappan ploughed field, (See page-2).

Plate II. Kalibangan, ploughed field on grid pattern, another view, (See page-2).

Plate III. Kalibangan, modern ploughed field on grid pattern with horizontal and vertical furrows, (See page-3)

Plate IV. Kalibangan, modern field with mustard and horse-gram plants in horizontal and vertical rows respectively, (See page-3).

space were sown horse-grams, while in the ones having greater spacing, it was the mustard plants (plate IV). The reason for such an arrangement also became clear: while the plant of the horse-gram is a short one, that of the mustard is tall and spreads out much more.

That the excavated field belonged to pre-Harappan times was amply clear. It was overlain by a layer of silt over which ran layers yielding typical Harappan material. These latter layers were also connected with Harappan structures close by (cf. plate I). In another part of the trench, the furrows were disturbed by clay enclosures and ash-pit carrying Harappan material (plate II). There was, therefore, little doubt about the stratigraphical position of the field. Carbon-14 determinations show a date between 2450 and 2300 B. C. for the pre-Harappan levels at Kalibangan. However, experts apprehend that the Carbon-14 dates for the second and third millennia B. C. may be younger by a few centuries. If that be so, the Kalibangan field may broadly be placed in the first half of the third millennium B. C.

As far as the present writer is aware, this is the earliest agricultural field so far excavated anywhere in the world.

GULF OF OMAN : THE ORIGINAL HOME OF INDIAN MEGALITHS

S. P. GUPTA

THE PROBLEM

The problem of the original home of the Indian megaliths has long been baffling the scholars. This is so in spite of the fact that most of the evidences point to their original home beyond the western borders of Afghanistan. The reasons for this difficult situation are primarily three:

(i) The typology of the megalithic monuments in India, as well as in the western countries, is extremely varied, so much so that we do not get all of the types at a single site or even in a single geographical or political zone; in fact, in every country there are several local types.[1] (ii) The grave-offerings in the megaliths outside India are also varied and we do not get in any country the repertoire similar to that found in India, although the parallelism of individual objects have been noticed in areas from Yemen to the Aral Sea and beyond.[2] In fact, each country has its own culture-complex associated with its megaliths. (iii) During the last two or three decades, most of the Western writers, and following them the Indians, have confined themselves to the consideration of those megalithic sites which are chronologically bracketed between 3000 B. C. and 1500 B. C. Obviously, these sites were either of the Neolithic period or of the Bronze Age.[3] Since the Indian megaliths belong to the Iron Age, the beginning of which was placed by Wheeler in the Achaemenian period,[4] a gap of thousand and odd years was repeatedly stressed by these writers. Obviously, the solution was nowhere in sight.

In the meantime another thread was picked up by Gordon who hinted at the possible relations between the southern Arabian cairn-burials and Baluchistan cairn-burials of the Iron Age.[5] This view was reiterated by the present writer;[6] it was, however, not accepted by some scholars including Banerjee,[7] who connected the Baluchi cairns with the Indian megaliths generically.[8] At the same time Heine-Geldern connected the Baluchi cairns with the Caucasian megaliths and the stone slabed graves of Tepe Sialk.[9] Recently, Leshnik has elaborated the Central Asian theory.[10] What is important to remember is that while Wheeler, Childe, Haimendorf,[11] etc., did not at all consider the Baluchi cairns as a link with the megalithic monuments of India, Banerjee,

Heine-Geldern and Leshnik looked upon them as the immediate source for the Indian megaliths, including those in south India.

A SUGGESTION

It is, however, difficult to believe that the Baluchi cairns or the Central Asian cists or cairns or barrows gave rise to the south Indian megalithic complex. On the other hand, it is strongly felt that the Baluchi cairns were generically related to the south Arabian cairns of the Iron Age. Of late, it has also been felt that the areas around the Persian Gulf or the Gulf of Oman may provide the key to the problem relating to the origin of the Indian megaliths. Belonging to the early Iron Age of the first millennium B. C., we have in that region, besides cairn burials, several types of sepulchral monuments,[12] the plans and the construction of which are reflected in the Indian peninsular megaliths whose traditions go back to the early Ist millennium B. C. Thus, south-eastern Arabia, with its outlet in the Gulf of Oman, may be taken as the epicentre of the Baluchi cairns as also the peninsular Indian megaliths. It was in the Islands in the Gulf of Oman that several traditions from Palestine, Mesopotamia, southern Arabia etc., came, mostly along with traders, and got fused; the graves discovered in south Arabian sites have actually yielded items from these regions. Thus, through the natural outlet of the Gulf of Oman, the people seems to have moved out eastward following the traditional sea-route along the Makran coast. Following Glyn Daniel's[13] theory that in their diffusion the megalith builders often followed the same route repeatedly, over a long period of time, we would like to suggest that at one time, along the Makaran route, the megalithic tradition travelled up to the Western Ghats of India and at another time the cairn-burial tradition travelled to Baluchi Makran, and Sind, may be up to Kutch and Saurashtra, along the same route. In both the movements, the traditions moved into the hinterland, from the south to the north. We do not visualize the voyage across the high seas from the gulf to the Western Ghats, although its possibility cannot completely be ruled out. While moving in the interior of different regions, these people seem to have come into contact with the local people, as also others who themselves might have been coming from elsewhere. Thus, we may visualize the possibility of the Baluchi cairn builders occasionally coming into contact with the West Asian and Central Asian peoples and borrowing from them certain material items and spiritual ideas. Similarly, we can also visualize hybridization of the original ideas with those locally prevalent ones, leading to the new modified forms of the sepulchral monuments as also the mode of the disposal of the dead. However, *we do not have sufficient evidence as yet to connect the Baluchi cairns with either the Vindhyan or the peninsular (Indian) cairns generically,* although, as Wheeler says, 'ideas have wings' and they might have travelled into these lands in a casual way which is beyond our comprehension.

With this much of theoretical background regarding our theory, we come to the actual archaeological evidence in southern Arabia and Persian Gulf islands.

DATA

The explorations and excavations in these regions have brought to light the following types of sepulchral monuments, all datable between 1000 B.C. and A.D. 100. These are cairns, cairn-circles, rock-cut caves, menhirs, barrows, triliths, tumuli, terracotta sarcophagi, cists, etc. Some of these monuments bear Himyaritic inscriptions going back to 1000 B. C.

CAIRNS, CAIRN-CIRCLES AND CAIRNS WITH MENHIRS

In southern Arabia, we come across several types of cairns, e.g., round, oval, square and rectangular. Along the southern shores, at sites like Ras Resut, the "larger ones measured 6 to 12 metres in diameter and reached a height of about two-thirds of a metre above plain. Around the larger graves were smaller ones looped to their circumference".[14] The cairns, in a large number of examples, were 'cairn-circles', i.e., they were surrounded by either a single chain or double concentric chains of big boulders. It is important to note that in areas like the Hajar province of Hadhramaut a cairn is marked by a free standing menhir in its centre.[15]

It is significant to mention that many of these types of cairns are found in Iran and India; round and oval types have been reported from southern Iran, Baluchistan,[16] Gujarat,[17] the Vindhyas[18] and the whole of the peninsula;[19] square and rectangular cairns have been located in southern Iran,[20] and Sind,[21] and the Vindhyas;[22] and the cairns with menhirs have been discovered in Madhya Pradesh.[23]

ROCK-CUT CAVES AND BLACK-AND-RED WARE

In Hadhramaut, Aden Protectorate, on Wadi 'Amd, opposite town Hureidha, there are a number of rock-out tombs in the scree-slopes of the valley cliffs. Two of these graves—A5 and A6—have been excavated by Caton Thompson. They turned out to be round chambers with rock-cut benches along the cave walls. Tomb A5 yielded the skeletal remains of 42 individuals and a large quantity of grave-goods, kept in small groups over the floor as well as on the benches. The offerings consisted of 87 earthen pots, several beads, and a number of bronze and iron-bronze objects.[24] A6 yielded the bones of three persons, beads, earthen pots, a pair of seals, etc.[25] According to the excavator, following the opinion of Beck, the beads are of Eastern Mediterranean type of the 6th centrury B.C. and the seals are of the Achaemenian type.[26] Harding, on the other hand, dated the pottery to the 9th century B. C. He discovered similar pottery at Adiat-al-Sultan, in Eastern Aden Protectorate. The same pottery was again found in the lowest levels of Hajar-bin-Humaid, dated to the 9th century B. C. by C-14 method.[27] It appears, therefore, that the graves belong to the Ist half of the Ist millennium B. C. In connection with the offerings Thompson has made another significant observation; "···caravan or coastal traffic may have brought them (i.e., beads, seals, etc.) from the Persian Gulf."[28] Clearly, the Persian gulf was on the regular trade route between southern Arabia and the countries of Western Asia.

There has been another interesting discovery in the Hadhramaut Wadi at Mashgha. Here a big pot-sherd was found which was "red to black on the outside and black in."[29] The black-and-red ware might have come from Palestine.[30] In the Indian context it is associated with the cultures ranging from the Harappan period to the megalithic.[31] It may not be out of place to mention that Egypt had this ware at the grave sites of Tumas, etc., of the 2nd millennium B.C., i.e., in the porotohistoric times,[32] and Palestine might have got it from there. This Egyptian black-and-red ware of 'C' Group people of 2000-1000 B.C. also moved in Ethiopia[33] and it is equally possible that South Arabia got it from this country which was quite near. Although, I am not in a position to suggest that India learnt the technique of producing black-and-red ware from Egypt, or Ethiopia or southern Arabia, yet, as Sri B.B. Lal has very pertinently pointed out to me, in a personal discussion with him, that it may not be without significance that the black-and-red ware is found confined to a rather homogeneous land curve that may start from Egypt and fall in south India; it is not found in any other region of the ancient world.

In connection with plain pottery Allchin may be quoted: "Legged urns identical to Indian types are reported from the Yemen."[34]

In the Jebel Sot region, D. van der Meulen has made two important discoveries. One was a series of "well cut square columns of stone, about 1·2 metre high, and linked up two of these were flat stones set in a rectangle".[35] The other was a series of open rings of upright slabs.[36]

It may be pointed out that such menhirs have been reported from Asota in Baluchistan to the central regions of Kerala,[37] and slightly similar table stones have been brought to light in the tribal belt in eastern India.[38] The 'open rings of upright slabs' remind us of the 'Hood Stones' from Kerala.[39] It may, however, be made clear that the east Indian 'Table Stones' are likely to have been related with the south-east Asian complex and not the Western complex since the prehistoric cultures of eastern India had always the south-east Asian bias.

TERRACOTTA SARCOPHAGIUS

Terracotta sarcophagi, sometimes with anthropomorphic lids (e.g., at Sankarvaram) and sometimes without legs (e.g., at Maski) have been reported inside and outside the megaliths from Kerala to Madras. Since such pottery coffins were not in use in India in the pre-Megalithic context, it has repeatedly been suggested that it came from Western Asia: in Mesopotamia it was in use from 3000 B.C. (at Baghadad[40] several oblong and short legged sarcophagi were found); in Palestine its use has been attested to even in the Iron Age (at Beth Shan and other places they are dated to 1200 B.C.); in Egypt its tradition goes back to the chalcolithic times, but it is important to note that Canaanites used them even in 900 B.C.[41] It may here be pointed out that this tradition was alive even in the Persian Gulf round about 900 B.C. Glob excavated one such sarcophagus in the Bahrain island. It belonged to the Neo-Babylonian times and it yielded three arrowheads and one dagger of iron, seven rings of copper, a seal stone, etc.[42]

TRILITHS OR 'TOPI-KALS' (?)

In northern Jol, Meulen has reported another interesting discovery, that of a 'trilith'. It "consisted of three long stones, about a metre high, standing on end and leaning towards each other. Sometimes a trilith had a fourth small stone on top. Occasionally, a series of triliths was enclosed with an elliptical line of pebbles."[43] In the interior of Oman, Thesiger has reported a number of triliths and tumuli in some sites on the banks of Ithli, in wadi 'Amairi, near the western end of Jebel Salakh and Andam.[44]

A trilith is not identical with a '*topi-kal*', which has four stones, but those with cap-stones and stone-circles might have inspired the form of a *topi-kal*.

CISTS AND JAR BURIALS

In the island of Qatar, Glob explored a cemetery of about 50 cairns usually measuring ten metres in diameter and one metre in height. He opened one of these cairns and found "a stone cist with roofing slabs, surrounded by smaller boulders. The cist lay in a north-south direction and was cut down into bed-rock".[45] It measured 1·9 metres in length. The monument seems to belong to the middle of the 2nd millennium B.C., i.e., the latest phase of the chalcolithic culture of the island.

Interestingly enough, on a rock nearby, hundreds of 'cup-marks' were found. According to the excavator they 'undoubtedly represent the female sexual characteristic'.[46] While interpreting the cup-marks on the circle-stones of Junapani, Rivet-Carnac compared them with the Morse code.[47] Such cists, cairns and cup-marks are known to us from the Vindhyas to the Deccan.

It may also be mentioned that at places like Ras Abaruk and Mezru'ah in the island the graves continued to be erected till the 3rd century B. C. They have yielded iron swords and arrowheads, glass objects, pot-sherds of the early Seleucid period, etc.[48]

In the Bahrain island, along the north coast and outside the extensive Bronze Age cemeteries, there are a large number of cairns and barrows of the Iron Age. Tumulus no. 36/2 is their typical example. It was oriented east-west and it contained the secondary remains of an adult and a child along with a silver bracelet, iron dagger and knife.[49]

At Ras-al Matbakh a large jar burial has also been reported.[50]

Allchin writes: "Stone-cist graves, with or without port-holes, are found in the Levant and on the coasts of Arabia."[51]

SOME TOPOGRAPHICAL OBSERVATIONS

About the topographical setting of the megalithic cemeteries in south Arabia Philby has made some very significant observations since most of them are equally applicable to the setting of Indian megalithic grave-yards. He writes: "the evidence of more plentiful water in these parts in ancient times argues the presence of a large agricultural and pastoral community in the vicinity of the cemeteries those days, while the analogy of Kharj province accounts for the burials on higher ground away from the habitation ...I would offer a suggestion that in them we have a link with the Phoenicians of old."[52]

The south Indian megalithic sites are also generally found situated near tanks and on a higher ground, away from the habitation. Similarly, the types of iron tools from the graves also prove that the people were partly nomadic-pastoralists and partly agriculturists. However, we may or may not agree with the Phoenician theory of Philby.

THE CAMEL VIS-A-VIS THE HORSE IN MEGALITHS

In one of the south Arabian graves, excavators have discovered the fragmentary bones of the camel.[53] As against this in some of the Baluchi cairns[54] and Peninsular graves[55] fragmentary bones of the horse have been found. Naturally, the question may be raised that if southern Arabia had anything to do with either the Baluchi cairn burials or the peninsular megaliths, why do we not get the camel bones in them ? Further, how to account for the association of the horse with the cairn and the megalith builders ?

One may place any number of suggestions, alternatives and arguments in favour or against a theory in this regard, but one simple fact need not be forgotten: the two animals have their own habitats, each absolutely different from the other; the camel is a desert animal but not the horse. Obviously, the camel was of no use to most of the people in peninsular India. Moreover, it has repeatedly been pointed out by all the authors that by-and-large, the megalith builders, during the process of their diffusion, took with them what we now loosely call 'megalithism'—i.e., the plan and structure of the monument, the system of collective burial, etc.—and not the culture-complex. If the migration was coastal, which seems to be largely so in the case of megaliths, even the mount, and that too a camel, was not taken to the new region; generally it was hardly feasible. The migrating people adopted the culture-complex and the popular mount of the local people. Moreover, let it also not be forgotten that so far camel bone has been found only in a few graves in south Arabia and, therefore, is not of much statistical value. But then the other question is more significant. How to account for the association of the horse with the Indian megaliths and cairn burials ? One of the probable answers may be that the animal in question, both in Baluchistan[56] and in penisular India,[57] is likely to have existed prior to the newcomers. If so, the migrating people simply made greater use of this animal than hitherto. It is possible that the people were inspired to do it because of two reasons: firstly, their coming into contact with the Iranian and the Central Asian hordes while moving hinterland in Baluchistan, and secondly, the compelling necessities of a nomadic people on the march.

However, the existence of the domesticated horse in India prior to 1000 B. C., i.e., in the Harappan, Chalcolithic and Neolithic times, has as yet not been convincingly proved; at least the archaeological evidence quoted so far is far from conclusive.[58] On the other hand, the horse was certainly put into use by the people of Western and Central Asia much before this date.[59] This important evidence leads to two conclusions: firstly, at least a few groups of the cairn builders of Baluchistan as well as the megalith builders of peninsular India were in close contact with those adept in breeding the horse in captivity. These horse-breeders could be either Iranians or Central Asians. If they were Iranians, they could be from the Fars, as they could be from any other place. I am thinking of the province of Fars in south-eastern Iran because we have a number of cairn burial sites in that region. Secondly, at least one group of the megalith builders may also have migrated along the land-route although the evidence at present is slender.

What could be the land-route through which the horse came to India round about 1000 B.C. ? If it came through the Fars, it could have taken the southern route across southern Baluchistan, Sind, Gujarat and the peninsular region but if it came from northern Iran, i.e., from the region of Sialk, it could have entered into the Zhob valley, Swat Valley, Indo-Gangetic plains and the peninsular regions. But such routes are only broadly so; when the diffusion of an important item like the domestication of the horse takes place its movement is more radial than unidirectional. It means, once it came to Baluchistan at any particular place soon it diffused in all directions, covering practically the whole of Baluchistan in a short time. Similarly, when it entered the Indo-Gangetic plains it was diffus d in all directions quickly. As a matter of fact, it is likely to have entered into these plains from several points in the north as well as in the south. Since the diffusion of the horse must have been the 'Trait Diffusion', i.e., accompanied or unaccompanied by items of material culture, it is not possible at the present state of our knowledge to work out the diffusion of the horse in the context of a particular culture-complex and a particular route.

The megalith-builders, travelling along the Makran coast (which does not mean that they were always in the boats), could have acquired the knowledge of domesticating the horse anywhere in southern Iran; of course, in the present state of research 'where' and 'how' this knowledge was acquired cannot be answered.

This discussion is based on the popularly held assumption that the horse came to India from western Asia. But it should not be forgotten that Arabia has always been famous for the good breed of the horse. But how early it appeared in south-east Arabia is not known although by about 1700 B.C., or slightly later, the horse was known to the Kassites in Babylonia and Syria, the Mitannis on the upper Euphrates, the Hittites in Asia Minor, the Amorite principalities of Palestine and the New Kingdom of Egypt. Zeuner, however, feels that it came to India with the Aryans in the middle of the 2nd millennium B.C. from northern Iran.[60] If it is so, the Megalithic folk were not responsible for introducing the horse in India. But Zeuner's theory is based upon linguistic evidence alone; archaeological evidence does not take back the horse in India prior to 1000 B.C. The introduction of the horse seems to be coeval of the introduction of iron.

STONE CISTS IN SAUDI ARABIA

The Danish expedition of 1964 also explored limited area in Saudi Arabia. In the small island of Tarut, about two miles from the town of the same name, Glob and Bibby discovered several stone cists and "around these, and on the surface of the mounds, lay quantities of fragments of alabaster and steatite vessels apparently of first millennium B.C."[61]

CAIRNS WITH PORT-HOLED SLABS IN OMAN PENINSULA

Danish archaeological expeditions in the Oman peninsula have explored a number of round mounds with port-holed and plain megalithic graves of the Bahrain cairn type surrounded by stone-circles of the period between the third millennium B.C. and thirteenth century B.C. The type site is located between villages Hili and Qatara on the northern edge of the Buraimi Oasis which lies about 200 km. hinterland from Abu Dhabi. The corresponding habitation site is securely dated to the period between the 3rd millennium B.C. and 12th century B.C.[62] In the region between Al-'Ain and Jebel Hafit several cairns and tumuli were excavated, some of which have been dated to the 13th-14th centuries B.C. on the basis of a Luristan type bronze sword.[63] It may, therefore, be reasonably presumed that in the Oman peninsula the megalith builders might have lived up to about 1200-1000 B.C. (C-14 date : SM 1113=3196±156 B.P.) It is possible, though not Proved, that around 1000 B.C. these people, along with others, living in Aden Protectorate as well as round the Gulf of Oman and the Persian gulf, slowly moved out towards the east along the Makran Coast. Halting and marching, imbibing many new elements and leaving behind several old ones, yet holding fast to the practice of megalithism, they reached the Western Ghats of India.

CONCLUSION

The above quoted evidences are based upon the extremely limited explorations and excavations conducted in southern Arabia so far; more work will certainly throw fresh light on the problem. In this short space I have tried to put at one place some of the relevant factual data known uptil now. They are fragmentary and expanding. They hardly convey any unified story; what we do not know is much more than what we know. Any one can see that the similarities shown above are extremely distant; there is not a single example where we may have an exact prototype of the Indian megaliths. The caves in the Hadhramauṭ Valley are round and with rock-cut benches, but they have neither the central pillar nor the central opening, nor the vertical and side entrances, nor the antechambers, etc., of the Indian rock-cut caves of Kerala. The sarcophagi in Baghdad, etc., are hardly so much elaborate with a large number of elephantine legs with holes, vaulted lids, etc., as they are in India. The 'triliths' in south Arabia is much different from the 'topi-kals' of Kerala. The Bronze Age cairns with portals are also not the typical port-holed cists of south India because the former has several arterial galleries within its construction. The black-and-red ware in south Arabia is so far represented by only one example.

Almost similar is the case with the Iranian, Palestinian and Central Asian examples quoted by a few authors. The so called port-holed cists of Sialk are long corbelled structures and not box like structures of the Indian types. The Palestinian examples are so much removed in time and space that they could not be the immediate source of origin for the south Indian megaliths. In typology also a number of examples of the Palestinian group do not find place in India, e.g , double-storeyed cists. The Central Asian examples of cairns, circles and mounds are also far removed in the richness of typology from the south Indian typology.

Obviously, one may ask for the grounds on which we correlate the Arabian and Indian examples. To us, they are only of the generalized kind: use of big stones, shapes of the receptacles of skeletal remains, presence of portals, ground-plan of the monuments, black-and-red ware, etc. Long back, Gordon Childe had also pointed out to these generalized similarities[64] However, *our deductions are extremely tentative* which may be discarded if something positively comes to light against it. But for the present, to us, the evidences appear extremely tempting in favour of the Gulf of Oman theory which seeks the origin of Indian megaliths is southern-eastern Arabia.

NOTES

1. Krishnaswami, V. D., "Megalithic Types of South India" *Ancient India* (hereafter abbreviated as *AI*), no. 5 (1949) , pp., 35-45; Daniel, Glyn, *The Idea of Prehistory* (Pelican books, Harmondsworth, 1964) ; Childe, V. Gordon, "Megaliths", *AI*, no. 4 (1947), pp. 4-13.

2. Soundara Rajan, K. V., "Megaliths and Black-and-Red Ware", *Seminar Papers on the Problem of Megaliths in India,* Memoirs of the Department of Ancient Indian History, Culture and Archaeology, no. 3, Banaras Hindu University, Varanasi, 1969 (hereafter abbreviated as *SPPMI*), pp. 76 ff; Ramachandran, K. S., "Megalithic Rock-cut caves and their parallels outside India", *SPPMI*, pp. 59 ff; Dikshit, K. N., "The origin and Distribution of Megaliths in India", *SPPMI*, pp. 5 ff; Allchin, B. and R., *The Birth of Indian Civilization*, (Pelican books, Harmondsworth, 1968), pp. 229-30; Leshnik, L. S., "Early Burials from the Nagpur District, Central India", *Man*, vol. 5, no. 3, pp.498 ff.

3. Childe (1947), *op.cit.*, Haimendorf, F., "The Problem of Megalithic Cultures in Middle India", *Man in India*, vol. XXV (1945), pp. 73-86; Wheeler, R. E. M., "Brahmagiri and Chandravalli 1947...........", *AI*, no. 4 (1947), pp. 181-308;

Krishnaswami (1949) *op. cit.*; Srinivasan, K. R. and Banerjee, N. R., "Survey of South Indian Megaliths," *AI*, no. 9, (1953), p. 108.

4. Wheeler, R. E. M., *Early India and Pakistan* (London, 1960), p. 24.

5. Gordon, D. H., *Prehistoric Background of Indian Culture* (Bombay, 1958), p. 18.

6. Mishra, V. N. and Mate, M. S. (Editors), *Indian Prehistory : 1964* (Poona, 1965), p. 205.

7. *Ibid.*, p. 214

8. Bannerjee, N. R., *The Iron Age in India,* (New Delhi, 1965), pp. 42-49.

9. *Ibid.*, p. viii, foreword.

10. Leshink, *op. cit.*

11. Haimendorf, *op. cit.*

12. Bowen. R. L., *Archaeological Discoveries in South Arabia* (Baltimore, 1958); Bowen, R. L. Jr., *The Early Arabian Necropolis of Ain Jawan* (New Haven, 1950); Bent, T., *Southern Arabia* (London, 1900).

13. Daniel, *op.cit.*, p. 100.

14. Bowen (1958), *op. cit.*, pp. 134-35. Also see, *Journal of the Bombay Branch of the Royal Asiatic Society,* vol. III, pts. I and II (1847-1856), pp. 262-63.

15. Bowen, *op. cit.*, p. 134. See also, H. Ingram, "Excursion into the Hajr Province of Hadhramut," *The Geographical Journal* (abbreviated *GJ*) no. 98, 1941, pp. 124 ff.

16. Gordon, *op. cit.*, p. 156.

17. Rao, S. R., "Excavations at Amreli," Bulletin, Museum and Picture Gallery, Baroda, (abbreviated *Bull. MPGB*), vol. XVIII (1966). The excavated site is Amreli. Rao kindly informs me that in central hilly regions also there are some sites. J. P. Joshi has also discovered at least nine cairns in Kutch at Sayakhan-ni-Wandh. They are circular in shape, about 2 metres in diameter. These rubble heaps were noticed on the slope of Nilwa Hills. (*IAR-1967-68*, p. 16.)

18. Carlylle, A. C. L., "Report on a Tour in East Rajaputana in 1871-72 and 1872-73", *Annual Report, Archaeological Survey of India,* vol. VI, pp. 13-15, 33-39, 88-89, 104-108.

19. Aiyappan, A., "The Megalithic Culture of South India,," *Indian Science Congress Association*, vol. XXXII (1945), Presidental Address.

20. Lamberg-Karlovsky, C. C., "The Cairn Burials of south-eastern Iran", *East and West*, NS, vol. 18, Nos. 3-4 pp. 269-76. The important excavated sites are

Sari-i-Asiab, Fanuch, Tump-i-Gabraha, etc.

21. Raikes, R., *Archaealogical Explorations in Southern Jhalawan and Las Bela,* (Rome, 1968), pp. 156 ff. The sites are Jeman Goth, Kanar, etc.

22. Singh, P., "Megalithic Remains in the Aravalis", *uratattva*, vol. 2 (1968-69), pp. 46-48. See also, G. R. Sharma, *IAR-1962-63,* p. 41; *IAR-1963-64*, p. 57. The important sites are, Satmas, Dausa, Kotia, etc.

23. Deo, S. B., "Megaliths in Maharashtra", *SPPMI* (1969), pp. 27-36. Dhanora is the typical site for such monuments. *IAR-1956-57*, p. 35.

24. Caton Thompson, G., *The Tombs and Moon Temples of Hureidha* (*Hadhramaut*), *South Arabia* (London, 1944), p. 65. See also, F. Stark, "An Exploration in the Hadhramaut and Journey to the coast", *GJ*, no. 93 (1939), pp. 7 ff.

25. *Ibid.*, p. 103.

26. *Ibid.*

27. Harding, G. L., *Archaeology in the Aden Protectorates,* (London, 1964), p. 31.

28. Caton Thompson (1944), *op. cit.*, p. 103.

29. Harding (1964), *op. cit.*, p. 42.

30. I have personally seen a few black-and-red ware sherds in the University museum of Jerusalem (Israel) in 1963. I was told that they belong to late chalcolithic period of Israel, but none could tell me anything about the site from which they came.

31. Lal, B. B., "From the Megalithic to the Harappa: tracing back the graffiti on the pottery", *Ancient India,* no. 16 (1960), pp. 4-24.

32. Lal, B. B., *Indian Arhaeological Expedition to Qasr Ibrim, Nubia, 1962* (Cairo, 1967), Published by the Department of Antiquities of Egypt. On page 117 he writes: "Again, it is probable, though not proved that there may be some link between the C–Group culture of Nubia and Megalithic south." Black-and-red ware, also called as black topped ware, has been found in Egypt from 4000 B. C. onwards (e. g., at Naqda). See also, *IAR-1961-62*, pp. 66-70.

33. Dikshit, K. N., "On Origin and Distribution of Megaliths in India," *SPPMI*, p. 10. He quotes Dr. H. Straube of the Inst. of Ethnography, Cologne, for this information. Straube has himself explored this pottery in Ethiopia. See also, Azais, R. P. and Chambrd, R., *Cinq Anneis des Rcheres Archaeologius en Ethopie*, (Paris, 1931). Quoted by Dikshit.

34. Allchin, B. & R., *The Birth of Indian Civilization*, p. 230.

35. Meulen, D. Van der, "Aden to Hadhramaut and Journey to the Coast", *GJ*, 93 (1939), pp. 122-23. See also, Bowen (1958) *op. cit.*, pp. 134-35.

36. *Ibid.*

37. Gordon, *op. cit.*, p. 183.

38. Haimendorf, C. von E., "Megalithic ritual among the Gadabas and Bondos of Orissa", *Journal of the Asiatic Society of Bengal* (abbreviated *JASB*), vol. IX (1943), pp. 149-87.

39. Krishnaswami (1949), *op cit.*, p. 40.

40. Jones, I. N. and Hall, J., *Jr. Bom. Branch of Royal Asiatic Society*, vol. IV (1853), p. 378.

41. See for details, Dikshit, *op. cit.*

42. Glob, P. V., "A Neo-Babylonian Burial from Bahrain's Prehistoric Capital", *Kuml* (1956), fig. 5.

43. Bowen (1958), *op. cit.*, p. 135.

44. *Ibid*; see also, B. Thomas, *Arabia Felix* (London, 1932), p. 126; See also, W. Thesiger, "Desert Borderlands of Oman", *GJ*, no. 116 (1950), p. 153.

45. Glob, P. V., "Prehistoric Discoveries in Qatar", *Kuml* (1957), p. 177.

46. *Ibid.*

47. Rivet-Carnac, J. H., "Prehistoric Remains in Central India", *JASB*, 1879, vol. XLVIII, pp. 1-16.

48. Madsen, H. J., "Arabian Gulf Archaeolgy", *Kuml* (1964), p, 104.

49. Bibby, T. G., "Five among Bahrain's Hundred Thousand Grave-mounds", *Kuml* (1954), 139.

50. Madsen (1964), *op. cit.*

51. Allchin, *op. cit.*, p. 230.

52. Philby, J. B., *Sheba's Daughters* (London, 1939).

53. *Ibid.*

54. Stein, Aurel, "An Archaeological Tour of Gedrosia," *Memoirs of. the Archaeological Survey of India*, no. 43, p. 88. In two of the hundreds of cairns at Gatti, the excavator found the skulls of the horse.

55. *IAR-1961-62*, p. 33; the horse's bones were found in a cairn circle at Junapani, near Nagpur. They were also found in a similar context at Khapa, near Nagpur. See, S. B. Deo, *Excavations at Takalghat and Khapa* (Nagpur, 1970), pp. 9 and 60-61. At Hallur, Nagarajarao found them in the Megalithic-Neolithic overlap levels of about 1000 B. C. (Allchin, 1968, *op. cit.*, p. 165).

56. Piggot, Stuart, *Prehistoric India* (Pelican books, Harmondsworth, 1952),

p. 121. Four teeth of the domestic horse (*Equus caballus*) were found in the lowest levels of Rana Ghundai (RG I). Piggot writes: "Nomadic, horse-riding herdsmen using the site as a camping-ground are suggested by the finds in RG I; an infant's skeleton was also found buried at this level." Zeuner, of course, feels that these teeth may be of hemiones (half-ass).

Horse skulls were found in two of the Iron Age Cairn burials of Zangian. On the contemporary Londo Ware pots, from sites like Shami Damb, Gushanak, Bit Damb of Bhagawana, Londo, the horse and horse with a rider (at Gushanak) have been found depicted in painted designs.

57. From the upper levels of Mohenjodaro the horse's bones have been reported. From Lothal, as also one from Mohenjodaro, a terracotta figurine has been identified as the representation of the horse. Zeuner feels that the animal may be onegar, i.e.. wild ass, still found in Gujarat.

58. Allchin (1968), *op. cit.*, p. 260. By 1700 B. C. the animal was widely in use in this part of the world.

59. *Ibid.*, p. 144.

60. Zeuner, F. E., *A History of Domesticated Animals* (London, 1963), pp. 318, 332-3.

61. *Kuml, 1965, p.* 150.

62. Karen Frifelt, "Archaeological investigations in the Oman peninsula, A preliminary report", *Kuml, 1968*, pp. 170-75. The following passages are relevant to our present study:

"At a time when we in Denmark were building dolmens and passage graves, while Egypt was raising its pyramids, the Oman peninsula, too, had its megalithic graves." [p 170]

"Close to the monumental tomb [the one Frifelt excavated in village Hili, the round mound was 12 metres in diameter with 'colossally heavy and unwieldy stone blocks' (stones were generally smoothed on one side) forming a port-holed cairn] at the foot of the mountain of low mounds with potsherds and stone chippings on their tops, some with a single stone slab or so sticking up above the surface, most of them undoubtedly the remains of comparable tomb structures. Even 3-4 kms. to the north, almost buried in the sand dunes which stream in across the plain from the west, the undoubted ruins of a plundered tomb were found." [p. 173]

The ancient habitational mound nearby yielded pottery, steatite pots, seals, etc., terracotta figurines and bronze arrowheads. The pottery (with black linear designs on fine red ware) from the deepest levels were comparable with those found in the Kulli culture of the 3rd millennium B.C. The same ware has also been recovered in the Bahrain island deposits of the same date, and Uman-an-Nar cairns in the island of Abu Dhabi. The same comparison exists in the associated terracotta animal figurines. However, the pottery as well as the parallel sided leaf shaped bronze arrowheads from the uppermost burnt (desertion) layers are comparable to those from the graves of Tepe Guran in Persia which are dated to the 13th century B.C. The date has been confirmed by two C-14 dates obtained on the charcoal samples from these layers: SM 1114=3403 ±161 and SM1113=3196±156 B.P. [About Tepe Guran excavations, see Tharne in *Acta Archaeologica*, vol. XXXIV, p. 133]

See for more details, *Kuml, 1965*, pp. 149-50. *Kuml, 1966*, Fig. 1 on page 75, text on p. 94

63. *Kuml, 1964*, p. 109.

64. Childe, *AI*, no. 4, pp. 4-14.

For the views expressed in the 'conclusion' I am most thankful to my colleague Sri K. S. Ramchandran because in my long discussions with him I found he holds views entirely different from those I have expressed here. He feels that the megalith builders had a high sea journey from the Red Sea to the Western Ghats. I have, as the editor of this Bulletin, asked him to contribute a paper putting forward his views for a healthy and fruitful discussion.

Excavations at Chirand : New Light on the Indian Neolithic Culture-Complex

B. S. VERMA

The recent excavations at Chirand, District Saran, Bihar, have thrown a new light on the Indian neolithic cultures. For the first time, a full-fledged neolithic culture has been discovered in the Gangetic basin. Till about 1968, Chirand was known only for its chalcolithic culture, but in the recent dig, taken-up primarily for collecting samples for C-14 dating, a neolithic stratum of 3·5 m. thickness has also been discovered. The culture is known mainly by an impressive collection of bone tools and decorated pots.

BONE TOOLS

By now a fairly large area (in two different trenches, one measuring 10 × 10 m. and the other 10 × 15 m.) of the neolithic phase has been exposed. Among the important antiquities recovered are the bone and antler implements (plates I & II). They include different types of celts, scrapers, chisels (from large to small sizes), hammers, needles, points, borers, awls, diggers, a shaft-straightner (*baton-de-commandment*), pins, styli, arrow-heads (both tanged and socketed), and many unfinished implements, e.g., the shoulder bone of an ox which seems to have been used as a shovel. Such a large variety of bone and antler implements has so far not been reported from any other single site in India, excepting, of course, Burzahom where the tool-typology is basically different.

BONE ORNAMENTS

The neolithic people also made bone ornaments such as pendants, ear-rings, bangles, discs, and combs. Miniature bone replicas of neolithic stone axes were used as pendants and tortoise bone and ivory were used for preparing bangles. A reel-shaped object having horizontal perforations, is also remarkable. The people, therefore, seems to have mastered the technique of making all types of tools and ornaments of bone, even by drilling big hour-glass holes.

POLISHED STONE TOOLS

Four neolithic celts, besides many other ground implements, such as hammers, have also been discovered. Similarly, a number of other rectangular tools, pestles, querns, balls, etc., have been found. The rocks used for making these tools were quartzite, basalt and granite.

MICROLITHS

It is significant to note that the microlithic industry was an integral part of the neolithic culture of Chirand just as they were in south India. The tool types include micro parallel-sided blades, scrapers, arrow-heads, serrated points, notched blades, points, lunates, borers, etc. In addition, a few geometric microliths have also been discovered. The materials used for these tools are chalcedony, chert, agate, jasper, etc. A number of nodules and cores of these minerals were also discovered. *It is noteworthy that not a single blade has the crested-ridge.* The frequency of cores and nodules indicates that the microliths were locally manufactured. It may be presumed that the nodules were collected from the bed of the river Son which is not far away from Chirand ; just a few kilometres from the site in the south-east direction there is a place known as Haldi-chapra where the Ganga meets the Son. Pebbles of different types of stones are found in the sand of the Son and this may be the source of the raw material for the neolithic folk of Chirand.

BEADS

A good number of long tubular, long barrel, short barrel, cylindrical, triangular, disc-shaped beads of chalcedony, agate, jasper, marble, steatite and faience with an excellent finish were recovered from these excavations. Some of the beads were unfinished which indicates that they were locally manufactured.

TERRACOTTAS

Terracottas of humped bull, bird figurines, *naga* figurines (one is of the coiled variety), bangles, beads, punctured decorated objects (one shaped like a miniature *linga*, and the other like a barrel) and balls are very common. Two partially broken pieces of rectangular pendants with incised and punctured decorations are very interesting. One of them, with a hole in an applied knob in reverse for pinning, nicely resembles a modern brooch used by ladies. A small perforated stem, probably of a smoking pipe (traces of soot are found inside), is another significant object in terracotta. Some terracotta wheels have been also discovered. One wheel-shaped object (without hole) with convex sides and flat edge was discovered from the habitation levels of this phase ; its exact purpose has, however, not yet been determined but it is likely to have been used as a dabber. A few terracotta discs with central holes, which were probably used as spindle-whorls, have also been discovered. Many burnt clay pieces (with finger impressions) in different sizes have also been found but their exact purpose is not at all clear. They are, however, somewhat parallel to the oval terracotta akesc from Kalibangan.

CERAMICS

The pottery of this period is, by and large, handmade, although a few examples might have been made by using the 'turn-table' method also. The bulk of the pottery is in red ware, although grey, black and black-and-red wares were also used. It is important to note that even in the neolithic time people knew the inverted firing technique to produce the black-and-red ware, but the pottery forms or types are quite different from the chalcolithic black-and-red ware pots and pans. A considerable number of pots had fine lustrous burnishing on the outer surface ; the inner surfaces being mostly rough and hard brushed. The people showed excellent advancement in ceramic techniques as the types included vase with broad mouth and narrow neck, spouted vase, bowl, lipped bowl, perforated bowl, footed bowl, oval bowl with broad lip, bowl-with-stand, begging bowl, footed cup, channel spout, miniature pot, spoon or laddle; a knobbed pottery was also made by them. A miniature hand-made dish in red ware, which has double perforations on its four cardinal points, like a toy balance used by children, has also been discovered. The neck portion of the vases was highly burnished while the bases were rusticated. Applied decoration on the neck portion of the vase was however, very common. This technique was developed to conceal the butting of the neck with the body of the vases. Post-firing scratch decoration was also done on some of the pots, such as a wheel with hub and sixteen spokes. On one of the sherds there is a mat impression which definitely proves that they knitted mat out of some kind of reed.

One of the interesting characteristic features of the pottery was the post-firing paintings in red ochre on grey ware, and rarely on red and black-and-red wares. Only the linear designs were common : criss-cross design in groups of five lines, concentric semi-circles, wavy lines, etc., have been found on the pot-sherds. On one sherd, there is a painting in dots representing a *trisula*. Rim based painting was equally popular (Fig. 1).

STRUCTURES

There is some indication that in the early phase people lived on floors prepared below the ground, although they may have been roofed over. Later, we find them living on ground level floors with reed walls plastered with mud. A circular paved floor was discovered from the late phase of this period which was about four metres in diameter. A semi-circular hut was provided with several oblong ovens, probably for community cooking. It may be mentioned that outside this circular platform, post-holes were located at regular intervals. A fairly large number of burnt chunks of clay with reed or bamboo impressions have also been discovered from these strata, suggesting that the houses perished in some conflagration.

FOOD AND AGRICULTURE

It is apparent that rice was known to the people as paddy-husk impressions have been noticed on some burnt-clay pieces. It has further been confirmed by the discovery of a few examples of charred rice along with other charred cereals like wheat, *moong*, *masoor*, and barely. However, the people were not pure vegetarians as is evident from the discovery of a large number bones of animals, birds and fish, and clusters of fish-scales. The frequency of bone and lithic tools and weapons indirectly suggests that their main occupation was fishing and hunting. River shells and snails were also eaten by them since their remains have been found in great number. Opinion of the experts of the Zoological Survey of India on the remains of bones in the neolithic strata at Chirand has shown that the neolithic people had something to do with the elephant, rhinos, buffalo, ox, stag and deer, as the bones of these animals have been repeatedly found in different layers of the neolithic occupation.

CHRONOLOGY AND COMPARISONS

The Chirand neolithic complex, with its developed techniques in fabricating bone artefacts and beads, together with post-firing paintings in elaborate designs on pots, and highly burnished pottery, was certainly an advanced neolithic culture, perhaps without any knowledge and experience of metal working. Chirand is the only site in India which has yielded a neolithic deposit of more than three meters ; at Brahmagiri, Tekkalkota, Pikhilhal and Utnur the deposits vary between one to two metres only. Although calculating date on the basis of depth alone is hazardous, yet some useful guesses can be made since the deposit consists of repeated sequence of ashy deposits. Available C-14 dates for the neolithic phase range from 1900 B.C. to 1300 B.C. with the possibility of its beginning going back to about 2,000 B.C., if not earlier.

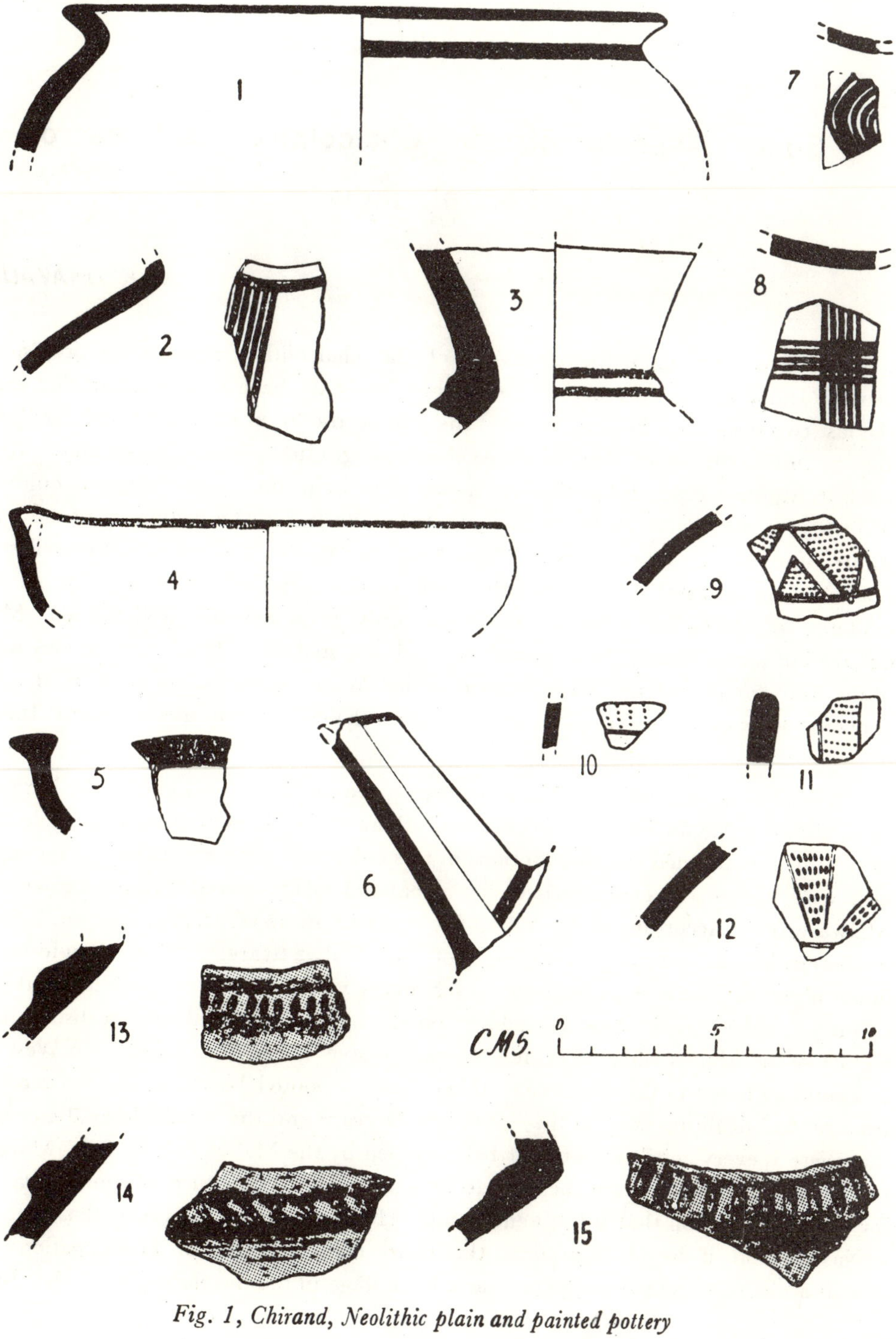

Fig. 1, Chirand, Neolithic plain and painted pottery

Some Aspects of the Chalcolithic Cultures of Central India

M. K. DHAVALIKAR

Consequent upon the discovery of the chalcolithic phase in the prehistory of central India, a large number of chalcolithic sites have been discovered in that area in the last two decades. Besides, some of these have also been excavated and, as a result, the cultural pattern of the 'Dark Age' is now gradually becoming clearer. Recent work in Madhya Pradesh has thrown a welcome light on the protohistoric cultures of Malwa stretching back the beginning of settled life before the beginning of the second millennium B. C. It was thus far held that the Malwa culture was the earliest that flourished in central India, but the new evidence affords conclusive proof of the existence of yet earlier cultures which not only preceded the well-defined Malwa culture but also probably contributed towards its making. Besides, some new aspects of the Malwa culture itself have been revealed by recent excavations. It is, therefore, proposed to examine the recent evidence on the chalcolithic cultures of central India.

Several aspects of the Malwa culture were brought to light by the large-scale excavations at Navda Toli by Sankalia and others in the fifties.[1] Subsequent explorations have amply established the distribution of this culture in time and space The culture, as is well known, is characterised by a painted black-on-red ceramic known as the Malwa ware. According to Sankalia, West Asian, more especially Iranian, influence is discernible in several pottery forms of the Malwa ware.[2] There should be little doubt about the extraneous influence, for many vessels have no parallels within the country. However, the channel-spouted bowl which is supposed to be a distinguishing feature of the Malwa ware does not appear to have been introduced from West Asia. It should be noted in this connexion that channel-spouted bowls have been recovered from several neolithic sites in the southern Deccan[3] and the available evidence shows that there is every possibility of their being copied by the Malwa culture folk. Moreover, this form of spout cannot be said to be a characteristic feature of the Malwa ware for the simple reason that it is absent at such Malwa culture sites as Kayatha, and even at Navda Toli it begins to occur in the third cultural phase of its occupation. The idea of a channel-spout thus appears at a later stage in the development of the Malwa culture. Although Sankalia's[4] suggestion of its West Asiatic origin is plausible it can nevertheless be stated that vessels with channel-spout are not uncommon at neolithic sites in the southern Deccan. In fact a careful study of the pottery from such sites as Brahmagiri, Tekkalkota, Piklihal, Sangankallu, T. Narsipur, etc., shows that the channel-spout probably evolved from the lipped bowl through the short channel.

The recent excavations at Kayatha show that the Malwa ware can be classified into two distinct fabrics. The pottery so far found at sites like Navda Toli and others is rather thick in section and coarse in fabric; the core is usually unoxidized. The vessels in this ware are treated with a thick silp over which painted ornament is executed in a dark brown-to-black pigment. The repertoire of designs is extremely varied and includes geometrical and animal and plant motifs. In sharp contrast to this thick coarse ware, we come across a *de luxe* fabric which is a variety of the Malwa ware. This has been found in considerable quantities at Kayatha and could therefore be classified as a distinct fabric. It should be mentioned that at Eran this finer fabric of the Malwa ware is abundant and it therefore deserves the sobriquet 'Eran Ware'. It is represented by the shapes similar to those in the Malwa ware and so also is the case of the painted motifs. It appears to be a characteristic industry of eastern Malwa. However, nothing can be said about its distribution in eastern Malwa where intensive exploration has yet to be carried out. But it should be stated that this fabric is also present at Navda Toli, though in small quantities.

The excavations at Eran conducted by the University of Saugor have yielded, according to the excavator, a new ceramic industry of the chalcolithic period.[5] It has been labelled as the painted grey ware which, however, should not be confused with the iron age pottery of the same name which occurs in north India. The painted grey ware of Eran is said to have been exactly similar to the Malwa ware so far as the fabric, the shapes and the painted patterns are concerned. The writer had an opportunity of examining the pottery of the Eran excavations through the kind permission of Professor K. D. Bajpai. It was noticed that the so-called painted grey ware was not a distinct ceramic industry as has been made out by the excavator, but that it is only the Malwa ware. On closer study it becomes apparent that some of the vessels of the Malwa ware turned greyish in parts because of the variation in firing conditions in the kiln. Similar sherds, grey in colour, have also been found at Kayatha and Navda Toli. It may not be out of place to mention here that even in Jorwe ware we find several sherds, nay complete vessels, which are brownish grey in colour. It would therefore be proper to classify the grey ware from Eran as the Malwa ware.

A very important feature of the Malwa culture which was so far unknown has been revealed by the excavations at Kayatha. A large number of terracotta figurines of a singularly unique variety were found in the course of excavations. They comprise only animal figures among which the most predominant are the bulls. They are divisible into two distinct categories on stylistic grounds, that is, naturalistic and stylized. Both are made of extremely fine clay, free from impurities of any sort, and all are uniformly well-baked. No figurine is treated with slip of any kind, nor is there any attempt at ornamentation. The only decoration, if one can call it that, consists of nail marks over the body of animals. This, though somewhat rare, recalls to the mind similar treatment on some of the Harappan terracottas.[6] On several specimens we clearly see the finger impressions of the hands that fashioned them. The delicate modelling is evident in the long pointed horns; the hump is most prominent and the mouth pinched, while the block-legs remind us of similar treatment of protohistoric figurines from other parts of the country.

Of the naturalistic rendering there is nothing that is especially noteworthy; it is the stylized forms of bulls which deserve special attention. There are several varieties of the stylized forms. In a majority of cases the head with horns and the conspicuous hump are present but the whole hind part is absent and, in its place, we see a stem, with a rounded end; sometimes the end is flat and this serves as a pedestalled base for keeping the figurine on a platform during the ritual. The degree of stylization reaches a new mark in the form that depicts a pair of short horns on a stem or pedestal. Such horns at once remind us of the bull cult of the Minoans in whose palace at Knossos in Crete we come across several representations of a pair of horns. But it is only a family resemblance and beyond that no relationship can be hazarded.

The naturalistic and stylized forms of bulls are found together and, even among the latter, all the different varieties occur right from the beginning, thus precluding any attempt at tracing the evolution of different forms. The stylized bull forms are unique inasmuch as they have no parallels elsewhere in the country even later in the historical period and they therefore remain an enigma. They have been found in considerably large numbers and therefore seem to have been used as votive offerings; they also might have been suspended in the neck by means of thread as the Lingayats do at present. The bull cult has a hoary antiquity in India where the beast is worshipped even today.

It is rather enigmatic that the terracotta bull figurines, more particularly the stylized forms, should be absent at other sites of the Malwa culture. However, it appears that they have been found at some sites, but have not been identified as such, as they were too fragmentary. Thus a good number of terracotta animal and human figurines have been reported from Eran. Of the published ones, two appear to be the fragments of stylized bulls.[7] Of these, one is a short stemmed with flat end and having a long curved horn; the other horn is broken. The other representation consists of a pair of short horns on a stem with rounded end. Stratigraphically they belong to the earliest pariod of occupation of the site, but have been grouped with human figures.[8] The comparative rarity of the stylized bull figurines at other sites in central India is betoken of the popularity of the cult in western Malwa, more particularly in the Chambal valley.

Thus far the Malwa culture people were supposed to be the pioneering colonizers of central India. However, the recent excavations at Kayatha have yielded extremely important evidence showing that the Banas culture flourished in western Malwa even earlier. Explorations in southern Rajasthan have established the focus of the Banas culture in the Banas valley and it appears that it also spread in the adjoining regions of Madhya Pradesh. All the diagnostic traits of this culture, such as the white-painted black-and-red pottery, are present in western Malwa. But the evidence from Kayatha shows that, at least in central India, it was not purely a copper age culture but was a chalcolithic culture characterised by a specialized blade-flake industry of chalcedony and other silicious material while at the same time copper or bronze appears to have been extremely scarce. It is obviously due to the absence of suitable copper ores in Malwa, and the people therefore had of necessity started the production of lithic tools on a massive scale in order to adapt themselves to a new environment.

Another characteristic feature of the Banas culture which has been revealed by the Kayatha excavations is the stylized bull figurines. The figurines which have already been referred to in connection with the Malwa culture are actually a distinguishing feature of the Banas culture in central India. In fact it is the Malwa culture folk who borrowed the idea of the stylized bull figurines from the Banas culture people together with their white-painted black-and-red ware. As already observed, the figurines of bulls are both naturalistic and stylized. It is again enigmatic that the stylized forms of bulls should have been absent in the original home of the Banas culture, but should occur in the peripheral zone. However, a close examination of the evidence from such excavated sites of the Banas culture as Gilund and Ahar in Rajasthan shows that such bull forms are not totally absent. They could not be identified as they were too fragmentary and also insignficant in number. Thus at Gilund a fragmentary terracotta object which has been takan to be a gamesman actully appears to be a bull form.[9] So also is the case of two figurines from Ahar.[10] This would show that the stylized bull forms from Kayatha are not totally absent in the Banas valley.

The stylized bull forms have no parallels in India and even beyond the frontiers of the country. But surprisingly enough a strikingly similar form is reported from Anau in south Russia.[11] The excavation report, however, does not contain any information regarding such bull forms except that it is a figurine of a horned animal. But the Anau specimen is far removed from the Indian in point of time and it is therefore not possible to hazard any relationship between the two. However, it may be noted that Sankalia has shown Western Asiatic contacts with the Banas culture as is evidenced by the similarity between the terracotta spindle whorls bearing incised decorative patterns.[12] The bull forms may therefore be taken as yet one more link between the Indian and Western Asian cultures.

The discovery of the Banas culture in Malwa has no doubt stretched back the antiquity of the settled life in central India to the first quarter of the second millennium B. C. But the discovery of a new culture shows that the first farmers of central India settled here even before the beginning of the second millennium. The culture has been named after the type site Kayatha (District Ujjain, Madhya Pradesh) where it was first discovered by V. S. Wakankar. He also excavated some trial trenches at the site on behalf of the Vikram University, Ujjain. The evidence from his excavations appeared to be significant and hence excavations were planned by Dr. H. D. Sankalia and conducted by the writer and Dr. Z. D. Ansari under the asuspices of the Deccan College Post Graduate Research Institute, Poona, in joint collaboration with Sri Wakankar of the Vikram University.

The Kayatha culture has been found to be entirely different from any other chalcolithic culture of the sub-continent. It is characterised by three distinct ceramic industries. The principal ware is a dark brown slipped pottery painted with designs in violet. The other is a red painted buff ware which is of extremely fine fabric The commonest shape in this ware is the typical Indian *lota* with a concave neck and a globular base. The third ceramic is what can be labelled as the 'Combed Ware' on account of its being decorated with incised design which appear to have been executed with a comb-like instrument. The decoration is, however, confined to the exterior of vessels only. The predominant shape is an open bowl. The pottery at once recalls to the mind the incised ware from pre-Harappan levels at Kalibangan. But the latter bears the incised decoration on its interior.

The foregoing analysis of the evidence from recent excavations in Malwa amply shows that the beginning of the settled life in central India can now be stretched back well before the opening the second millennium B. C. These pioneering colonisers can be taken to be the junior contemporaries of the Harappans. They disappear from the scene around 1800 B. C. We have presently no evidence to know either their whereabouts or their antecedents. They are suceeded by the Banasians who are characterised at least in central India by their bull cult. The Malwa culture people borrowed the bull cult of the Banasians. The finer fabric of the Malwa ware which has been named herein as the 'Eran Ware' bears some resemblance with the red painted buff ware which is a charactristic ceramic industry of the Kayatha culture and it is therefore not unlikely that the latter contributed towards the making of the Malwa culture. This, however, is a tentative hypothesis which remains to be confirmed by concrete evidence. Such evidence can be furnished by a site possibly in the Chambal valley where there is a clear-cut overlap between the Kayatha and the Malwa cultures. It may help us to some extent in tracing the origin of the Malwa culture.

The bull cult of the Banasians in Malwa is another enigmatic problem. But on deeper thought it will be revealed that a people of the same culture and stock can have different religious beliefs. The parallel that immediately arises to the mind in this case is the mother goddess cult which was so predominant in the Indus cities of Harappa and Mohenjo-daro but was conspicuously absent at Kalibangan and Lothal.

Equally enigmatic is the end of the Malwa culture. At several Malwa culture sites, such as Kayatha, there is a clear break in the occupation of the site. These sites were deserted by the Malwa culture people about 1300 B. C. They remained unoccupied for about six to seven centuries and were again inhabited in sixth century B. C. For the solution of this problem the key site appears to be Nagda where there is supoosed to be an overlap between the chalcolithic and the early historic times. This may become clear when the fuller report of the Nagda excavations is published. Be that as it may, the mosaic of the cultural pattern of central India during the second millennium B. C. is gradually emerging clear as a result of the recent work.

Notes

1. Sankalia, H. D., Subbarao, B. and Deo, S. B., *The Excavations at Maheshwar and Navadatoli, 1952-53*, Deccan College and M. S. University of Baroda, Publication no. 1, Poona-Baroda, 1958.

2. Sankalia, H. D., "New Links between Asia and India of 4000 years: Excavations in the huge "Dust Heap" of Ahad, near Udaipur," *The Illustrated London News*, September 1, 1962, pp. 322-25.

3. Sarma, I.K., "Painted pottery from Pusalpadu, Andhra Pradesh and further explorations in the Cuddapah and Kurnool Districts," *Indica*, vol. IV (1967), no. 2, pp. 79-94.

4. Sankalia, H. D., "Spouted vessels from Navda Toli (Madhya Bharat) and Iran," *Antiquity*, vol. XXIX (1955), no. 114, pp. 112-14.

5. Singh, U. V., "Further Excavations at Eran," *Journal of the Madhya Pradesh Itihasa Parishad*, vol. V (1967), p. 21.

6. Mackay, E. J. H., *Further Excavations at Mohenjo-daro*, in two vols. (Delhi, 1938), vol. II, pl. LXXX, 12.

7. *Indian Archaeology 1962-63—A Review* (hereafter, *IAR)*, pl. XXXIV A.

8. *Ibid*., p. 11.

9. *IAR-1959-60*, p. 43, pl. XLV A, 2.

10. Sankalia, H. D., Deo, S. B., and Ansari, Z.D., *Excavations at Ahar (Tambavati)* (Poona, 1969), p. 194, fig. 117, no. 4 and 118, no. 2.

11. Pumpelly, Raphael (Ed.), *Explorations in Turkestan—Expedition of 1904: Prehistoric Civilization of Anau*, in two vols. (Washington, 1908), vol. I, p. 172.

12. Sankalia, H. D., "New Light on the Indo-Iranian or Western Asiatic Relations between 1700-1200 B. C.," *Artibus Asiae*, vol. XXIV (1963), nos. 3-4.

Mammalian Fossil Fauna : a most modern tool for dating the Pleistocene deposits

E. KHAN

Archaeologists, as far as I understand, study man, his cultures and the tools which he prepared in various environments he lived during the prehistoric times. Within the span of this time he invented numerous techniques in the preparation of tools which matched properly with the environments. Thus for thorough understanding of the background for invention of various techniques, close study of the environment is a must, and for this the biota (fauna and flora), climate, soil/rock and morphology of the region are investigated comprehensively as the environment is the sum total of the effects of these forces among themselves. It has also to be investigated whether the numerous techniques evolved gradually in different parts of the world or they developed simultaneously in the same region or in far off areas; and for solving this the palaeontological and radiometric methods are very helpful. Thus, the field of archaeology appears wide enough to be studied by a group of scholars specialised in different branches mentioned above. The aim of the present paper is to throw light on how the knowledge of the mammalian palaeontology helps to determine the geological age of the Pleistocene deposits where tools may also occur at their factory sites or after being transported from there.

HISTORICAL RUSUME

Leaving aside all that has been done on the Pleistocene, it will be appropriate to start from the work of De Terra and Paterson who tried to give a comprehensive account of India during the Pleistocene period by the study of glaciation, terrace formations, fluvo-lacustrine deposits, fauna, including early man, and the tools he used.[1] According to these authors the beginning of the Pleistocene period which is synchronous with the commencement of the first glaciation, is recognised in India at the base of the Tatrot beds, and other Indian Pleistocene deposits have been correlated after accepting it. This view is still held by many Indian archaeologists and palaeobotanists. But mammalian palaeontologists revised this view in the 18th International Geological Congress held in the Great Britain,[2] and agreed that Blancan

(USA), Villafranchian (Europe), Pinjaurs (India), and Djetis beds (Java) marked the beginning of the Pleistocene equivalently. Later, by a detailed study of the fauna and the lithology of the Upper Siwaliks, east of Chandigarh, it has been recognised that the Lower Boulder Conglomerate is equivalent to Gunz[3] and other Indian Pleistocene deposits have been correlated on this basis. Recently a new correlation chart of the Indian Pleistocene deposits has been given.[4] (Fig. 1)

METHODS OF CORRELATION AND AGE DETERMINATION

The degree of fossilisation was sometimes considered as a valid criterion for distinguishing the old from the young age bed. But it has now been widely recognised that the fossils collected from the younger sandstone beds were more fossilised than those from the older clay beds. Even the degree of fossilisation in sandstone beds of the same age from different localities is not the same if the conditions for fossilisation at two places differ.

It has also been observed that with the passage of time flourine and nitrates, etc., gradually accumulate in the fossils. Thus it was presumed that the high percentage of these in the fossils collected from a bed would be older than the bed or beds whose fossils show low percentage of these. Later experience proved that the high or low percentage of these items does not indicate the geological age of the bed. On the contrary, it presents the high or low percentage of these items in the beds where the fossils come from.

Similar heavy mineral suits were used for correlating the beds. But it was discovered after considerable work that similar heavy mineral suits might be of different ages, whereas dissimilar heavy mineral suits might be of the same geological age. Thus, similar heavy mineral suits indicates similar source rocks rather than similar geological age.

Human artefacts have sometimes been used for determining the geological ages of the beds where they have been collected from. But it has been realised that they are not always *in situ* and mostly have come to rest there by way of transported material from factory sites.

K/Ar and C^{14} methods are very useful to find out the exact age of the rocks, directly and indirectly despite some discrepancies. But C^{14} method is not applicable for the rocks older than 60,000 years, and K/Ar method is unreliable for the rocks younger than 1,50,000 years[5], whereas the period from 1,50,000 to 60,000 years is very crucial for prehistorians. Under these circumstances only fossils can be helpful for correlation of the rocks and other geological formations of this period.

PALAEONTOLOGICAL METHOD

The purpose of the palaeontological studies is to date the rocks in which the fossils are found, and consequently to correlate the rocks occuring far apart from one another. Invertebrate fossils are used for correlating the Palaeozoic formations, when evolution and dispersal of these animals were rapid, and vertebrate fossils were inadequently known. Mainly reptilian fossils are relied upon for the correlation of the Mesozoic formations, and invertebrate fossils serve as supplements. Tertiary and Quaternary formations are correlated mainly on the mammalian fossils, when their evolution and migration were very fast, whereas those of invertebrate (except for micro-fossil) and reptilian were almost constant.

Despite the fact that during the 19th century vertebrate fossils were the only reliable source to date the Mesozoic, Tertiary and Quarternary formations, geologists rarely used them for correlation, and mostly depended upon the invertebrate fossils. This was only because of the rarity of the vertebrate fossils. Besides, their detailed morphological study demanded more time which geologists of that period could not afford. Naturally, the study of the vertebrate fossils was taken up by zoologists who did not care for the localities and horizons which yielded the fossils. Ultimately, vertebrate fossils became show-pieces of museums practically without any correlative use. During the period, the knowledge of the vertebrate palaeontology was developing and refining; geologists, finding the invertebrate fossils inadequate, resorted to other methods for correlations mentioned above. But as has already been said, invertebrate and reptilian fossils are not useful for correlative purpose of the Pleistocene period. Palaeobotany of this period was also not much developed and refined for the determination of the age, except for ecological interpretation. Thus, in this connection, only mammalian fossils can be safely used since nearly all large forms of the Pleistocene period are thoroughly studied with respect to their temporal and spatial distribution.

A brief summary of how it has been achieved is given below with reference to Indian works only to maintain brevity.

In the first half of the nineteenth century vertebrate fossils were collected in India with great enthusiasm and their brief descriptions mostly appeared in the journals of the Asiatic Society of Bengal, but specific localities were not mentioned, and passing reference to the geological age was made. The last phase of this type of work is that of Falconer.[6] Lydekker[7] took up detailed description of the specimens

Fig. 1. SUMMARY OF CHRONOLOGICAL PLEISTOCENE EVENTS IN INDIA

AGE	DE TERRA & PATERSON (1939)		SANKALIA (1962)	
	JAMMU & PUNJAB	CENTRAL INDIA		CENTRAL INDIA
Holocene	T 5	T 5=Cotton Soil		Dry, New alluvium chalcolithic Dry, silt (upper clay) Microlith & survival of Middle Palaeolithic tool type
IV glaciation	T 4, loam silt and gravel Reddish loam	T 4=Pink clay (upper silt)	Late Pleistocene	Wet, gravel (Upper gravel) Middle Palaeolithic or late soan and rolled Lower Palaeolithic Abbevillio-Acheulian
III inter-glacial stage	T 3, Degradation (Soan industry)	T 3=sand (upper gravel)	Middle Pleistocene	Dry, silt (lower clay), developed Lower Palaeolithic, Fresh Acheulian Hand axes and Flakes
II glaciation	T 2, Potwar loessic silt, ±350 ft. (Soan industry)	T 2=Pink clay (lower silt)	Middle Pleistocene	Wet, gravel (lower gravel) Lower Palaeolithic Abbevillio-Acheulian
II inter-glacial stage	T 1,Upper Terrace gravel (Chello-Acheulian and Early Soan Cultures)	T 1=Conglomerate and sand (lower gravel)	Middle Pleistocene	Dry..........................
II glaciation	Erosion, tilting, Boulder Conglomerate zone±2000 ft. Boulder gravel in fan formation (oldest Flake industry)			
I inter-glacial stage	Pinjore zone±2500 ft. Pink silt and sand, Early Pleistocene fauna of Upper Siwaliks		Early Pleistocene	
I glaciation	Tatrot zone, conglomerate and sand, Upper Siwalik fauna		Early Pleistocene	Wet, Primary laterite
Early Pleistocene				
Upper Pliocene				

SAHNI & KHAN (1964)		KHAN (1968)	
PUNJAB (Simla Hills)	NARMADA VALLEY	PUNJA (Simla Hills)	NARMADA VALLEY
T 5	? Break	T 5	Black Cotton Soil
T 4	Upper silt	T 4	Narmada Channel=Hiatus
T 3	Upper gravel	T 3	upper silt upper gravel lower silt lower gravel (Lower & Middle Stone Age tools)
T 2	lower silt	T 2	lower gravel ?
T 1	lower gravel	T 1	?
Upper Boulder Conglomerate		Upper Boulder Conglomerate	?
Break		Hiatus ?	
Lower Boulder Conglomerate		Lower Boulder Conglomerate	
Pinjaur		Pinjaur	
Tatrot		Tatrot	

briefly described by earlier workers. He paid special attention to mentioning the localities but was not very careful about horizons. Pilgirm[8] was very particular of the horizons which yielded fossils. For this purpose he himself made fresh collections from the Potwar region and rejected all earlier collections which, in his opinion, were admixture of various horizons.[9] Thus, he, for the first time, established well founded correlation of the Siwaliks based on assemblage of fauna. Matthew[10] challenged the correlation put forwarded by Pilgrim, and emphasised that appearance of new species is a better criterion for correlation than that based on the assemblage of fauna, which indicates more of ecological environments rather geological age of the beds. Pilgrim modified his previous view to a great extent.[11]

Recently, the Upper Siwaliks around Chandigarh has been thoroughly investigated,[12] and for the first time a definite line of demarcation has been drawn between the Tatrots (Upper Pliocene) and Pinjaurs (Lower Pleistocene) on the basis of the appearance of new species. Very recently the author[13] visited the Narmada alluvial deposit, and also checked the fossils collected earlier from there. He has come to the conclusion that the age of the deposit ranged between 1,20,000 to 60,000 years, and the implements are unreliable to determine the geological age of the deposit since they are not at the factory sites but have been transported there from such sites. *In his opinion the Early Man reached Central India during the third glacial age.*[14]

The above conclusion has been drawn on the basis of mammalian fossils whose knowledge has been refined to such an extent that K/Ar data are checked with the age of the beds determined through mammalian fossils[15]

To elaborate the above point further it is better to explain it by the examples of some fauna fossils.

Stegodon :—The earliest species (*S. clifti*) of this genus is known from the Dhok Pathan stage (Middle Pliocene). This species is replaced by another advanced species (*S. insignis-ganesa*) during the upper Pliocene (Tatrots) and a further advanced species (*S. pinjorensis*) becomes common during the lower Pleistocene (Pinjaurs). Naturally, a more advanced species is expected from the Narmada alluvial deposit. But the species of *Stegodon* common in the Narmada fossil collection is recognised as *S. insignis-ganesa* whereas this is highly misleading. This is so only because the Narmada fossil collections have not been revised by any competent palaeontologist, and the result is that the mistake made in the early days has been repeated. It has been the practice during early days that new species were established on isolated teeth, whereas it has been proved beyond doubt that the characters of the skull should be taken on the whole, and no over-emphasis be laid on the characters of the isolated teeth, which are subjected to variation depending upon the age, sex and individual variations.[16]. Clearly, till complete skull of *Stegodon* is unearthed from the Narmada alluvial deposit the fossils should not be identified beyond generic stage. Recently, it has been claimed that *Stegodon* did not exist during the period the Narmada alluvial deposit was laid down[17] but a molar of the genus has been collected by the same author from there (Geology Museum, Panjab University). Moreover, most of the photographs of the fossils have not been properly arranged by Khatri to show the characteristic features of the species or even of the genus.[18] I am of the opinion that we in India urgently need publications with detailed and correct study and more photographs than hitherto available.

Hypselephas hysudricus.—The earliest fossil of this species is known from the Pinjaurs (Lr. Pleistocene), and it seems that this genus originated from *Archidiskodon planifrons* which itself orginated during the lower part of the Upper Pliocene. A variant of *Elephas namadicus* has similar teeth characters as those of *H. hysudricus*, and the finds of isolated teeth compelled the earlier workers to recognise them as those of *H. hysudricus*. This mistake has been repeated since those days, and recently even the skull of *E. namadicus* has been incorrectly identified as *E. indicus*.[19] The author studied almost all the material in the British Museum, Museum of the Geological Survey of India, Geology Museum of Panjab University, and came to the conclusion that the teeth recognised as those of *H. hysudricus* actually belong to *E. namadicus*, after taking into account the morphological characters of the skulls on the whole to which teeth of such characters are attached, and the distribution of *H. hysudricus* and *E. namadicus* in space and time.

Bovidae.—The sub-family of Bovidae can be identified with some degree of certainty, even on the basis of isolated teeth. But it is nearly impossible to distinguish the genera of the same sub-family on the basis of such teeth. Till complete skulls are found, species of the same genus cannot be separated but it has been the general practice that all the specimens of bovids, found in the entire Narmada alluvial deposit are recognised as *Bos namadicus*, and even in a recent work[20] this has been followed. Thus it seems that the same species (*Bos namadicus*) persisted from the Middle to Upper Pleistocene without any specific change, whereas this, in general, is against the observations made world over about the mammalian fossil fauna of the Pleistocene period.[21] Unless all the specimens of *B. namadicus* in British Museum, Museum of Geological Survey of India and Geology Museum of Punjab University are restudied thoroughly, definite identification of incomplete skulls cannot be made.

The claim of Khatri[22] that the remains of *Bison* are found in the Narmada beds, is

FIG. 2. **SPECIES AND THEIR GEOLOGICAL RANGES**

Species	Upper pliocene	Pleistocene			
	Tatrot	Pinjaur	1st to 3rd glacial	3rd Inter-glacial	4th glacial
PRIMATES.—					
Papio sub-himalayanus	—	—			
Presbytis sivalensis			?—		
Presbytis entellus					—
CARNIVORA.—					
Mellivora sivalensis		—			
Ursus namadicus				—	
Crocuta sivalensis	—	—			
Hyaena crocuta					—
PROBOSCIDEA.—					
Stegodon insignis-ganesa	—	—			
Stegodon pinjorensis		—			
Stegodon (? *namadicus*)				—	
Mammuthus (*Archidiskodon*) *planifrons*	—	—			
Elephas (*Hypselephas*) *hysudricus*		—			
Elephas (*Platelephas*) *platycephalus*	—	—			
Elephas namadicus				—	
RHINOCEROTIDAE.—					
Rhinoceros sivalensis		—			
Rhinoceros karnuliensis					—
Punjabitherium platyrhinum		—			
Rhinoceros deccanensis				—	
EQIDAE.—					
Equus sivalensis		—			
Equus namadicus				—	
Equus asinus					—

Species	Upper Plocene	Pleistocene			
	Tatrot	Pinjaur	1st to 3rd glacial	3rd inter-glacial	4th glacial
HIPPOPOTAMIDAE.—					
Hexaprotodon sivalensis	—	—			
Hexaprotodon palaeindicus				—	
SUIDAE.—					
Sus hysudricus	—	—			
Sus (? namadicus)				—	
CAMELIDAE.—					
Camelus sivalensis	—	—			
GIRAFIDAE.—					
Sivatherium giganteum	—	—			
BOVIDAE.—					
Sivacobus palaeindicus		—			
Hemibos triquetricornis		—			
Hemibos acuticornis		—			
Leptobos falconeri		—			
Pro-bison debmi	—	—			
Bison sivalensis		—			
Bos namadicus				—	—
Bubalus platyceros		—			
Bubalus palaeindicus				—	—

baseless because it is based upon not only incorrect identification of the fossils but also author's inadequate knowledge of the distributton of *Bison* in space and time.

Now it should be clear that wrong identification of the specimen is wholly responsible for misleading determination of the geological ages of the deposits, whereas the correct identification gives extremely precise results.

GEOLOGICAL RANGE OF IMPORTANT INDIAN PLEISTOCENE MAMMALIAN FAUNA

It would be appropriate to mention here that the Siwalik Hills and Narmada Valley are famous for the mammalian remains of the Pleistocene period. Till very recently it was the general view that the remains of the mammalian fauna are found in India from the Lower to the Upper Pleistocene without any faunal break—the mammalian fauna of the Lower Pleistocene in the Siwaliks and those of the Middle and Upper in the Narmada alluvial deposits. But the author is of the view[23] that almost all the mammalian remains unearthed from the Narmada alluvial deposits are of the last interglacial age. *Thus, on the one hand, the mammalian fauna existing in India during the time from the first to third glaciation is unknown so far, and on the other hand, the fauna of the last glacial age is scantily recognised.* Till this knowledge is complete, actual geological ranges of the known Pleistocene mammalian fauna of India cannot be definitely found out. However, taking into account the origin, migration, evolution, distribution and geological ranges of the various mammalian fauna of the world, the geological ranges of the Indian Pleistocene mammalian fauna can be inferred with greater degree of precision by the experienced palaeontologists. For general guidance geological ranges of the various Indian mammalian fauna of the Pleistocene period is given below. (Fig. 2)

NOTES

1. De Terra, H. and Paterson, T. T., *Studies on the Ice Age in India and Associated Human Cultures,* Carnegie Institute of Washington, no. 493 (Washington, 1939).

2. Wadia, D. N., *et al*, "Report of the Committee on the Pleistocene", *Proceedings of the 18th International Geological Congress*, London, 1948 (1951).

3. Sahni, M. R., and Khan, E., "Stratigraphy, structure and correlation of the upper Shivaliks, east of Chandigarh", *Journal of the Palaeontological Society of India,* vol. 4, pp. 61-72, 1964.

4. Khan, E., "Pleistocene Stratigraphy in India" *Annals of the Department of Geology, Aligarh Muslim University,* (hereafter *ADGAMU*) vol. 4, pp. 61-72, 1968.

5. Ishida, *et al*, "The Plio-Pleistocene Series in Kinki District, Japan", *Journal of the Geological Society of Japan*, vol. 75, no. 4, pp. 183-95, 1969.

6. Falconer, H., *Palaeontological Memoir,* vols. 1-2, ed. Murchison, R. I., (London, 1868).

7. Lydekker, R., "Molar teeth and other remains of mammalia", *Pal. Ind.* (X), vol. 1 (1876) pt. 2; "Note on the pelvis of a ruminant frcm the Siwaliks", *Records of the Geological Survey of India* (hereafter *RGSI*), vol. 22 (1889), pt. 4, pp. 22-24.

8. Pilgrim, G. E., "Correlation of the Siwaliks with mammal horizons of Europe", *RGSI*, vol. 43 (1913), pt. 4, pp. 264-323; *ibid.*, "Are Equidae reliable for the correlation of the Siwaliks with the Cenozoic stages of North America, ?" *RGSI*, vol. 73 (1938), pp. 437-84; *ibid.*, "The lower limit of the Pleistocene in Europe and Asia", *Geological Magazine,* vol. 81 (1944), pp. 28-38.

9. Pilgrim (1913), *op. cit.*, p. 265.

10. Matthew, W. D., "Critical observations upon Siwalik mammals", *Bulletin of the American Museum of Natural History,* vol. 56 (1929), pp. 437-560.

11. Pilgrim (1938) & (1944), *op. cit.*

12 Sahni and Khan (1964), *op. cit.*

13. Khan (1968), *op. cit.*

14. Khan, E., "Are mammals immigrant to India?", *ADGAMU* (1968), pp. 61-71.

15. Evernden, J. F., *et al*, "Potassium-Argon dates and the Cenozoic mammolian chronology of North America", *American Journal of Science*, vol. 262 (1964), pp. 145-98.

16. Khan, E., "Bio-stratigraphy and palaeontology of a Sangamon Deposit at Fort Ou' Appelle, Saskatchewan, Canada", *Publication in Palaeontology,* no. 5. 1970.

17. Khatri, A. P., "Pleistocene mammalian fossils of the Narmada River Valley and their horizons", *Asian Perspectives*, vol. 9 (1966), p. 130.

18. *Ibid.*

19. *Ibid.*

20. Tripathy, C., "Pleistocene alluvial deposits around Nevasa, Ahmadnagar District, Maharashtra", *RGSI,* vol. 95 (1968), pt.2, pp. 365-66.

21. Khan (1970), *op. cit.*

22. Khatri (1966), *op. cit.*, p. 123.

23. Khan (1968), *op.cit.*

An Appraisal of the protohistoric problems of the Ganga-Yamuna doab

R. C. GAUR

Sufficient material belonging to the protohistoric period has been brought to light in the Doab during last two decades. A proper assessment of the entire material is, therefore, necessary; particularly to determine the possible correlation between the various cultural deposits. Following cultural complexes have so far been unearthed in this region:

1. The Harappan or late Harappan
2. The Copper Hoard
3. The Ochre Coloured Pottery
4. The black-and-red ware
5. The Painted Grey Ware

Since the Harappan, the Copper Hoard and the O.C.P. complexes are more or less contemporaneous, it would be better if these three are examined simultaneously. Among the excavated sites of the Doab, Alamgirpur, on river Hindon in District Meerut, is alleged to be a Harappan site, representing a late or degenerate phase of the great civilivation.[1] Although several distinctive features are present to provide it its present nomenclature yet, it may be noted, the distinguishing characteristics of the Harappan civilization, such as big buildings, seals, evidence of writing, human figurines, etc., are conspicuous by their absence. On the other hand, if examined minutely, many new elements, foreign to the great civilization, may be seen in the excavated assemblage. Several pottery types, including vases with flaring[2] and out-turned[3] rims, vases with globular profile[4], basins with flaring and horizontal rim[5], knobbed lids[6], etc., are almost similar to those found in the O.C.P. industry. Paintings in black pigment, in the form of thick rim bands and parallel lines of varying thickness, are also common in both the industries. The incised device to decorate[7] the pottery, which was prevalent at Alamgirpur, is a typical phenomenon of the O.C.P. assemblage and not of the Harappan. An indeterminate crescent like object[8] having holes also looks similar to a terracotta object found at Lal Qila[9] in District Bulandshahar. All these features are worth considering, more so, when we know that the Harappans generally refused to learn innovations. Why then Alamgirpur presents such an assemblage ? In order to answer this question, representative cultural deposits both of the Sutlej and Ganga regions are to be examined carefully and minutely.

Of all the sites, Bara[10], in the Punjab, hardly 8 kms. from Rupar, is a typical site. Here two main phases—one representing a late phase of the Harappan culture and the other yielding certain new ceramic traditions including incised designs—were unearthed. Dr. Sharma[11] is, however, of the opinion, that seemingly Bara has, 'some affinity with the pre-Harappan Kalibangan and, although influenced by that tradition it still appears to be later than Ruper' (See elsewhere in this volume in the proceedings of the Seminar on O.C.P. *ed.*). His views more or less is corroborated by Deshpande.[12] According to him Bara 'may represent a reconciliation between the conquered pre-Harappan and the pre-Harappan Kalibangan. The people, when became conquered, moved in isolation and one finds their pottery with incised design'. While these presumptions have been made on the basis of the incised designs on the pottery, Cemetery 'H' influence on Alamgirpur has also been postulated[13], particularly on the basis of a few pottery types. Lastly, there comes its association with the O.C.P.[14] The writer of the paper recently got an opportunity to examine the Bara pottery afresh.[15] Resemblances seem to be present between Bara and Lal Qila complexes in the following types and decorative designs:

A. Pottery Types:

(i) Jars having splayed out rim, narrow neck, bulbous body and rounded base.

(ii) Dish-on-stand with short stem (?).

(iii) Basins with flat projection and undercut rim.

(iv) Vessels with rusticated surface.

B. Paintings:

(i) Fully painted neck of the pots havings horizontal single or multiple bands.

(ii) Hatched triangles.

C. Incised designs:

(i) Checked or compartmented designs.

(ii) Leaf pattern.

(iii) Wavy lines.

In the light of the above details, Bara seems to be a conglomeration of Kalibangan I, Harappan, Cemetery 'H' and the O. C. P. elements. It appears that Sutlej played an important role in the days of the late Harappan life. How and when the Harappans were forced to move to the Sutlej region and beyond in the northern and north-eastern zones of the western Punjab, is not known. This would perhaps have happened sometime around 1750 B.C. Not only the Harappan traditions travelled, but it seems that pre-Harappan traits also reached there. Though both the traditions appear to have survived in that region, their exact relationship in respect of time and influence cannot be determined at present.

However, the traces of Bara tradition have been noticed at several sites recently explored in the Sutlej basin.[16] Further eastward movement of the people to the Doab region is another noteworthy event of our protohistory. Bargaon[17] is an important station in this respect. Here we find the Harappan traits surving along with such pottery which have incised designs on both the sides, resembling those found in Kalibangan I.[18] However, Bargaon provides an interesting complex. I had an opportunity of handling the Bargaon material at Dehradun.[19] It has been observed during the study that the lower level was dominated by the Harappan pottery types; the middle level shows an overlap between the Harappan and the O.C.P. shapes; the upper level is mainly represented by the O.C.P. industry. However, the difference between the first two levels is not very distinct.

More than a hundred red ware sites belonging to the protohistoric period have been explored in the districts of Upper Doab, in U P., some of which have already been excavated. In is an interesting observation that none of these sites is devoid of the O.C.P. element. In fact, except Alamagirpur and the lower settlement of Bargaon, all the sites basically belong to the O.C.P. group. It has been observed that while the sites near the Punjab border in U.P. also include pottery shapes of the Harappan derivative or influence, those lying away eastward in the districts of Bulandshahar, Etah, Etawah and their neighbourhood, yield no such shapes and their assemblages bear distinct regional characteristics.

In the light of the above analysis the red ware industry of the Upper Doab[20] belonging to the protohistoric period may be classified into the following groups:

(i) *Genuine O.C.P. Sites:* Such as Atranjikhera, Lal Qila, Ahichchhatra[21], Hastinapur[22], Saipai[23].

(ii) *O.C.P. sites with Harappan influence*: Such as Bahadarabad[24], Ambkheri[25], Upper phase of Bargaon.

(iii) *Harappan sites with O.C.P. influence:* Such as Alamgirpur, lower phase of Bargaon.

It is now almost evident that the Harappan and the O.C.P. people belonged to two different cultural groups and were independent of each other. It also appears that the Harappan penetration in the Upper Doab was of temporary nature and devoid of its prosperity. The respective presence of the O.C.P. shapes at Alamgirpur and the Harappan shapes at Bahadarabad and Ambkheri also suggests that the peoples of the two cultures came in close contact with each other, at least for sometime, and borrowed, to some extent, the traditions of each other. These observations obviously pose the following questions:

1. What is the time bracket of the O.C.P. culture ?
2. What is the association of the O.C.P. and the Copper Hoards ?
3. Who were the authors of the O.C.P. industry ?
4. How and when the O.C.P. culture came to an end ?

Regarding the time bracket it is generally believed that the culture flourished sometime in the first half of the second millennium B.C.[26] This date has more or less been corroborated by the thermoluminiscent dating of a few pottery-sherds from Atranjikhera, Lal Qil, Jhinjhina and Nasirpur, determined by the Archaeological Research Laboratory at Oxford.[27] Of all these sites, Lal-Qila is the only undisturbed site. On the basis of the two dates available for the site, the O.C.P. culture may be placed here in the time bracket of 2030-1730 B.C. with a mean of 1880 B.C. However, other dates indicate that the culture-survived for a longer period at other sites. With this dating, the O.C.P. culture becomes almost contemporaneous with the Harappan Civilization. In this light, the whole problem has to be studied afresh.

So far as the relationship of the copper-hoards with the O.C.P. is concerned Lal[28] had already associated them with them O.C.P. people on the circumstantial evidences, as far back as 1951. Since then the hypothesis has gained further ground. Definite association of the copper with the O.C.P. has recently been established through a few excavations. A copper ring, familiar from Pondi and Bahadarabad, was reported from the reguler excavations at Bargaon[29]. A piece of copper and broken pieces of terracotta crucibles containing copper grains were found by me at Atranjikhera in 1965-66. However, of particular significance has been the discovery of the copper objects including an arowhead (?), a pendent, a bead and a broken piece of celt at Lal Qila. The association of the copper-hoards with the O.C.P. has further been strengthened by the discovery of a copper-hoard from an O.C.P. site adjacent to a village Kiratpur, on the

Kali Nadi, at a distance of about 3 kms. towards west from Lal Qila. This hoard includes an anthropomorphic figure, two celts, one of which has a five pointed star engraved on it, and rings or bangles. It is further reported that a sword and a harpoon, typical of copper hoards, have been dug out from an O.C.P. deposit at Saipai in district Etawah. This place had already yielded a big copper hoard in the past.

Since the association of the copper-hoards of the Doab with the O.C.P. has now been established the next problem is to determine the identification of the authors of the 'Copper-Hoard—O.C.P. culture'. Three hypotheses have been advanced:

1. They were the late or refugee Harappans.[30]
2. They were the indigenous people of the Ganga-Yamuna Doab[31].
3. They belonged to the Aryan stock[32].

As far as the first possibility is concerned, perhaps that has no validity now. It has already been discussed above that the Harappans and the O.C.P. people were independent of each other and were of two different stocks. The next comes their equation with the indigenous people. Who could they be ? The Austroloid ? No doubt, the cultural influences of the Austroloid group—ancient *Nishadas (?)* is still prevelent to some extent in our society. The spoke, probably, the *Munda* language. Many villages in Mirzapur District, from where protohistoric cave-paintings have been reported, derive their names from that language.[33] The Aryan penetration in the Ganga Valley, perhaps forced them to flee towards the south and south-eastern regions around the Vindhyan mountains. Later on though they were absorbed within the Aryan Society, they always constituted a different group within that fold as well. *Brihad-Devata*[34] calls them as the fifth *Varna.* But since the main spread of the O.C.P. culture was in the Upper Doab with extension towards the west, its identification with the Austroloid does not seem, at the present state of our knowledge, tenable. Then to which stock they belonged? The answer does not seem easy and perhaps cannot be answered at present. However, all available anthropological, linguistic and archaeological data must be taken into account before we accept or reject their identification with any aborginal group finally.

Lastly, comes their association with the Aryan stock. Each of the distinctive protohistoric remains, viz., the Harappan[35], the Black-and-red Ware, both painted and plain[36], and the P.G.W.[37] has at one time or the other been seperately associated with the Aryans. No attempt, however, was ever made to equate the O.C.P. people with any wave of the Aryans. But since the authors of the Copper-Hoard and the O.C.P. now appear as one and the same, a claim that was made for them much earliar by R.

Heine Geldern[38], of course, on different grounds, may again be considered. He had seen distinct western impact on the various Copper-Hoard tools. However, the observation, as pointed out by Lal,[39] perhaps, did not apply to the tools of the copper hoards found in the Ganga basin. But the possibility of their being the Aryans may not be shelved unless all the factores are analysed once again. Suffice to say at present that the co-existence of the Harappan and the Copper Hoard people with distinct entities and traits in the same region between the Sutlej and Ganga rivers and the presence of an anthropomorphic (?) figure in phase IV of Lothal belonging to circa 19th Century B.C. or a little later[40] do provoke searching analysis of the problem.

As far as the study of the black-and-red ware assemblage (Group no. 4) is conerned in this part of the country it is still in its infancy—nay in its embroynic stage. Its exact relationship has not yet correctly been determined with those found in the Banas valley[41] on the one hand those found in the eastern Punjab,[42], Haryana[43], eastern and nothern Rajasthan[44], on the other. It is significant to note that the black-and-red ware deposit as a separate cultural phase has so far been demarcated only at two sites, viz. Atranjikhera and Noh. The insignificant presence of the black-and-red ware industry at all the P.G.W. sites indicates that the industry was not a major component of the deposit. At Atranjikhera the pottery analysis[45] has shown that the black-and-red and Black-Slipped ware industries were in much better position in the earliest phase of the P.G.W. deposit and had out-numbered the P.G.W. industry itself. Gradually the P.G W. and the Grey ware improved their positions and they virtually ousted the other two potteries. The two then could survive only in name. This is indicative of the fact that the black-and-red and Black-Slipped wares were predecessors of the P.G.W. industry. But this is not the case with the sites excavated in the central Ganga valley, more precisely in the eastern part of Uttar Pradesh, such as at Prahladpur[46], Rajghat[47] Mason[48], Gularihwaghat[49]. A comparative study[50] of the cultural material from the black-and-red ware phase of these sites has clearly shown a general affinity among themselves and they all appear to belong to the Iron Age. The general characteristics of the cultural assemblages from these sites is nearer to the late phase of the P.G.W. deposit datable around 7th-6th centuries B.C. This fact has also been corroborated from the C^{14} dates. However, the black-and-red ware phase of Sonpur[51], further east in Bihar, comes probably from a pre-iron deposit. Be that as it may, there appears a great necessity of tapping more sites in the regions between Atranjikhera and Sonpur to have a clearer picture of the pre-iron black-and-red ware plain or painted, deposits more so when the industry continues in the Iron Age deposits. As far as the black-and-red ware industry of the Punjab and the eastern and northern Rajasthan is concerned, its association with the P.G.W. seems apparently proved, as both the wares have been picked up together during the course of explorattons. It is very likely that if some of these sites, as well as a few of western U.P., are excavated properly, a distinct phase of the black-and-red ware industry would come to light below the P.G.W. levels.

As far as the last group, namely, the P.G.W. industry is concerned, a detailed discussion was held at Aligarh Seminar in August 1968. The report is in the press. Since then no appreciable progress has been made in this direction and, therefore, I will prefer to exclude this group from our present discussion. However, the general consensus which emerged at Aligarh may be ennumerated here:

1. That the P.G.W. is an industry associated with those Aryans who lived during the Mahabharata period.

2. That its life span is likely to be roughly between 1100 and 500 B.C.

3. That the industry is indigenous one and has no affiliation whatsoever with any pottery outside India[52] of the ancient period.

4. That there is a great necessity of conducting horizontal excavations on a large scale of few selected P.G.W. sites in order to have an insight into the life of the Painted Grey Ware people.

However, it may be noted with great satisfaction that every now and then new sites[53] of the P.G.W. are coming to light, with the efforts of the devoted field workers, and the day is not far away when some of the major problems related with the P.G.W. will easily be tackled.

NOTES

1. *Indian Archaeology-A Review*, (Hereafter *I.A.R.*) 1958-59, pp. 50-52
2. *Ibid* , Fig. 24-28
3. *Ibid.*, Fig. 24-79
4. *Ibid.*, Fig. 24-13
5. *Ibid.*, Fig. 24-6
6. *Ibid.*, Fig. 24-14
7. *Ibid.*, Plate LXII, Period I
8. *Ibid.*
9. Lal Qila excavations were conducted by the Department of History, A.M.U; Aligarh, under the direction of the writer of the present paper.

10. *I.A.R.*, 1954-55, pp. 9-10, Plate XI.

11. Sharma, Y.D., *Archaeological Remains, Monuments & Museums*, Part I (Delhi, 1964), p. 9.

12. Deshpande, M.N., comments, *Indian Prehistory: 1964*: ed. Drs: V. N. Misra & M. S. Mate (Poona, 1965), p. 127.

13. (i) Allchin, B. & R. , *The Birth of Indian uivilization* (London, 1969), p. 149.
(ii Dikshit, K.N., "Nature of Harappan ware in Sutlej Valley", *Potteries in Ancient India* (Patna, 1969), p. 58.

14. Deshpande, *op.cit.*

15. The Bara pottery has been seen through the courtesy of Sri Y. D. Sharma.

16. *I.A.R.*, 1963-64, p. 17.

17. (i) *I.A.R.*, 1963-64 (ii) Deshpande, *op.cit.*

18. *I.A.R.*, 1960-61, 61-62, 62-63, etc.

19. The pottery has been seen through the courtesy of Shri M.N. Deshpande.

20. More O.C.P. sites are gradually coming to light from the lower Doab as well as from the adjoining areas of the upper Doab.

21. *I.A.R.*, 1964-65, p. 39.

22. Lal, B.B., "Excavations at Hastinapur and other Explorations..." *A.I.* no. 10-11, pp. 10-11.

23. (i) Thapar, B.K., "Methodology in Archaeology", paper read at the Indian Archaeological Society's Annual Conference, Nagpur Session, 1970.
(ii) Pottery seen through the courtesy of Shri B.B. Lal.

24. Sharma, Y.D., "Copper-Hoard and the ochre colour ware in the Ganga basin", paper read at the 1961 conference on Asian Archaeology, New Delhi.
(ii) *Archaeological Remains, Monuments & Museums*, p. 12.

25. (i) Deshpande, *op. cit.* (ii) *I.A.R.*, 1963-64.

26. Gaur, R.C., comments, *Indian Prehistory: 1964*, pp. 142-45.

27. Information from David Zimmerman, Oxford. Letter addressed to Prof. S. Nurul Hasan, A.M.U., Aligarh.

28. Lal, B.B., "Further Copper Hoards—A Review of the Problem", *A.I.*, no. 7.

29. cf. Krishna Deva, "Problem of the Ochre Coloured Pottery", *Potteries in Ancient India*, *op. cit.*, p. 77. (ii) Deshpande, *I.A.R.*, 1965-66, 66-67.

30. (i) Ghosh. A., "The Indus Civilization...", comments, *Indian Prehistory: 1964*
(ii) Rao, S.R., comments, *Potteries in Ancient India*, p. 80.

31. (i) Lal, *op. cit.* (ii) Gupta, S.P., comments, *Potteries in Ancient India*, p. 66. (iii) Gaur, *op. cit.*

32. Heine Geldern, R. (i) "Archaeological Traces of Vedic Aryans", *Journal Indian Society of Oriental Art* no. 4, 1936 (ii) "The coming of the Aryans and the end of the Harappan culture": *Man*, 1956.

33. *Linguistic Survey of India* vol. IV, p. 9. See also, S.P. Gupta, "Indian Copper Hoards...", *Jr. Bihar Research Society*, vol. XLIX, 1963, pp. 137 ff.

34. *Brihad-devata:* Vol. I. 453.

35. Ramchandran, T.N., *Presidential Address, Ind. Hist. Cong. Sec* I, Agra Session, 1956.

36. (i) Sinha, B. P., "Black-and-red ware and the Aryans", *Ind. Hist. Congress*, Alig. Sess. 1960 (ii) cf. Sharma, G.R., *The Excavations at Kausambi*, (Allahabad, 1960), pp. 10-13. (iii) cf. Sankalia, H.D., and others, *The Excavation at Maheshwar and Navadatoli* (Poona, 1958), pp. XIII and 2 to 4.

37. Lal, *A.I.*, no. 10-11. Also, *Presidential address: Seminar on the Painted Grey Ware*, Aligarh, 1968.

38. *op. cit.*

39. cf. Lal, *A.I.*, no. 7

40. Lal, *Indian Archaeology Since Independence* (Delhi, 1969), p. 19. Also, S. P. Gupta, "Further Copper Hoards, a Reassessment...", *JBRS*, vol. LI (1965), pp. 1-7.

41. cf. Sankalia, Deo, Ansari, *Excavations At Ahar* (Poona, 1969).

42-43-44. *I.A.R.*, 1956-57; 57-58; 58-59; 62-63; 63-64; etc. Dikshit, "A note on the Problem of the Plain Black-and-red Ware in India", *Pott. in Anct. Ind.*, pp. 48-55.

45. Gaur, Paper on P.G.W. Assemblage, Aligarh P.G.W. Seminar, 1968. (In Press).

46. cf. Narain, A.K., & Roy, T.N., *The Excavation at Prahaladpur* (Varanasi, 1968).

47. *I.A.R.*, 1960-61, 61-62, 62-63, 1963-64, etc.

48. *I.A.R.*, 1964-65, etc.

49-50. Roy, T.N., "The Pre-Northern Black Polished Ware Deposit", paper read at P.G.W. Seminar, Aligarh, 1968.

51. Verma, B.S., "Black-and-red ware in Bihar", *Potteries in Ancient India* pp. 102-11.

52. Ghosh, A., "A note on the Homeland of the Painted Grey Ware", paper read at Aligarh P.G.W. Seminar 1968.

53. *I.A.R.*, 1962-63, 63-64, 64-65, 67-68, etc.

NOTES & NEWS

A BONE AND ANTLER INDUSTRY FROM ALLAHAPUR, DISTRICT MEERUT

INTRODUCTION

The ancient mound of Allahapur,[1] about 13 kilometres west of Muradnagar in U.P., lies on the left bank of the river Hindon, a tributary of the Yamuna. The nearest village is Surana. The excavation of the site was taken up in order to augment our knowledge about the culture-complex of the Painted Grey Ware using people. In all, fourteen layers revealed an occupational deposit of about 2·80 metres, which was broadly divided into two periods. The excavations not only confirmed the nature of the Painted Grey Ware complex encountered at other sites in the Ganga-Yamuna Valley but also added a new factor: the preponderance of the plain black-and-red ware over the Painted Grey Ware during the early phase (IA) of the occupation of the site (layers 13 and 14). Significantly enough, the shapes of the black-and-red ware and Painted Grey Ware are the same. It seems probable that the Painted Grey Ware phase at Allahapur flourished for a longer period in comparison to other sites in the Upper Ganga-Yamuna doab since it clearly overlaps with the Mauryan levels. The excavations at Allahapur also revealed a variety of bone objects such as arrowhead,[2] stilus and awl. They require a detailed techno-typological study because these objects have not been encountered in the past in such a large number from any of the Painted Grey Ware sites.[3] It is significant to note that 90% of these objects are manufactured out of antlers. The presence of a number of unfinished objects indicates that the tools were locally made, a fact which may also show that it was a village of bone-tool makers who supplied the tools to other nearby settlements.

TECHNIQUE OF MAKING TOOLS

The technological studies of the bone implements found in the Painted Grey Ware complex at Allahapur allow us to work out different stages[4] of their manufacture. The simplest method of working antler,[5] a solid bony out-growth arising from the frontal bones of male species, generally, was to select a particular point where it was to be broken. It was first charred over fire and then the charred place was scraped with a sharp tool. Thus the notch produced penetrated through the compact layer into the spongy matter below. Now it could be broken without any difficulty. It may, however, be pointed out that several examples are available where a notch was obtained even without firing the area in which the point of weakness was to be created.

In some parts of Maharashtra[6] (specially in the Ratnagiri District), a few centuries ago, a portion of bison horn was kept moist with coconut oil and heated on a fire until it became as soft as wax. It was then worked, or pressed into the required form, either with hands or in moulds made of hard wood. The object was finished off with scraping tools and a small lathe. The linear ornamentation seems to have been executed by a fine, double pointed graving tools of iron. The few tools found are extremely simple: a thick small wire with a flattened end. They are also likely to have used a small rude lathe, a fine saw a few triangular blades without handles (for scraping and polishing), three or four graving tools of different sizes, with a file or rasp. Even in modern times[7] antlers are boiled in hot water before they are cut by sophisticated specialised saws.

A few unfinished points from Allahapur shed a valuable light on the successive manufacturing stages (Plate III). There are evidences to show that antler, in a number of examples, was first charred over fire. After removing the desired piece (from the main horn) from the central part of the charred portion, the chopping was roughly done at one end for preparing the tool. First the tang was made, then the blade body was dressed up to the desired shape anb size. Thus, once the whole body has been roughly brought out, probably with the help of a few metallic implements, the object was subjected to burnishing and polishing. First the blade was tackled and then the tang.

MICROSCOPIC EXAMINATION

The microscopic studies[8] revealed some important clues regarding the mode of fabrication of bone tools. The bone-antlers were rendered soft by keeping them in hot water for sometime. In some cases coconut oil was used to soften the structure. As the tissue are hygroscopic in nature, they absorb the liquid in which they are immersed and become soft. In the present case, a few antler pieces were burnt as is evident from the carbonization of the outer surface, then they were dipped in suitable softening medium, and finally cut to the desired shape by the use of fixed crude lathe which could have been made of iron. On one of the implements there are regular concentric lines over the whole body. They appear to have been made by some sharp pointed crude lathe type of contrivance and as the lines of cut were made in a more or less

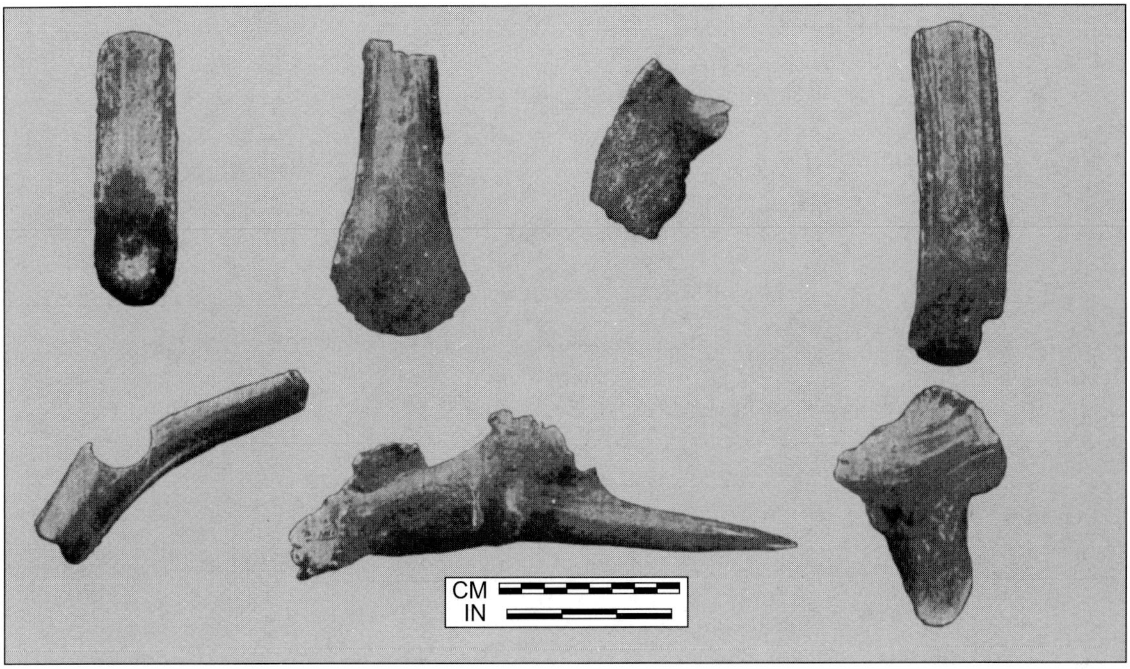

Plate I. Chirand, Neolithic bone axes, baton-de-commandment, etc., (See page-19).

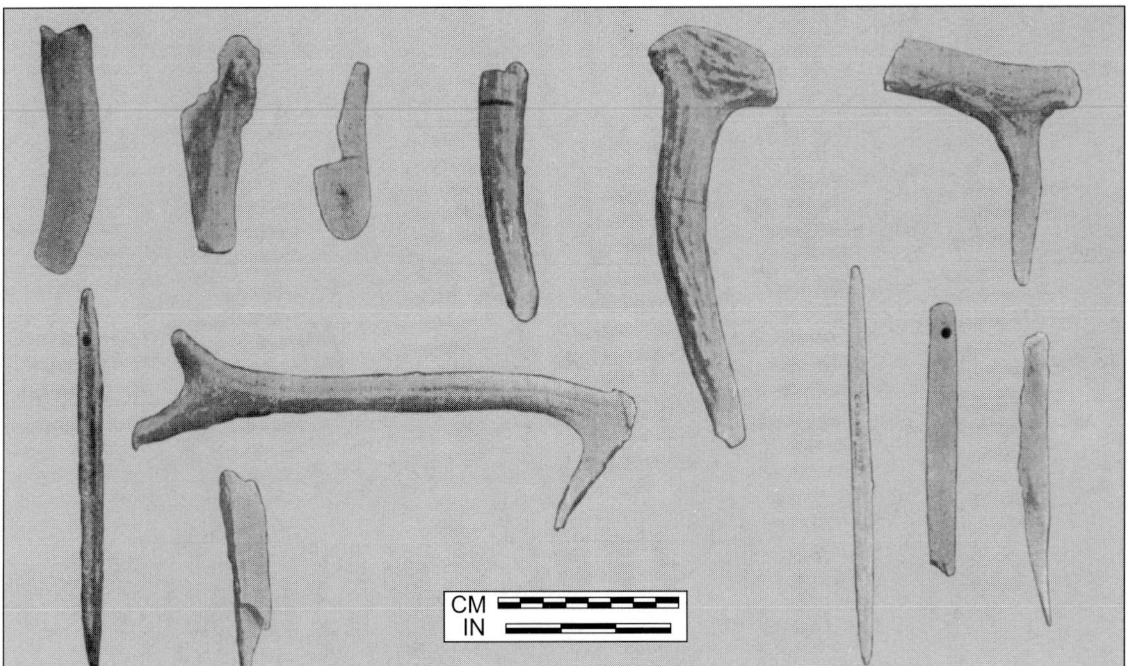

Plate II. Chirand, Neolithic bone implements, (See page-19).

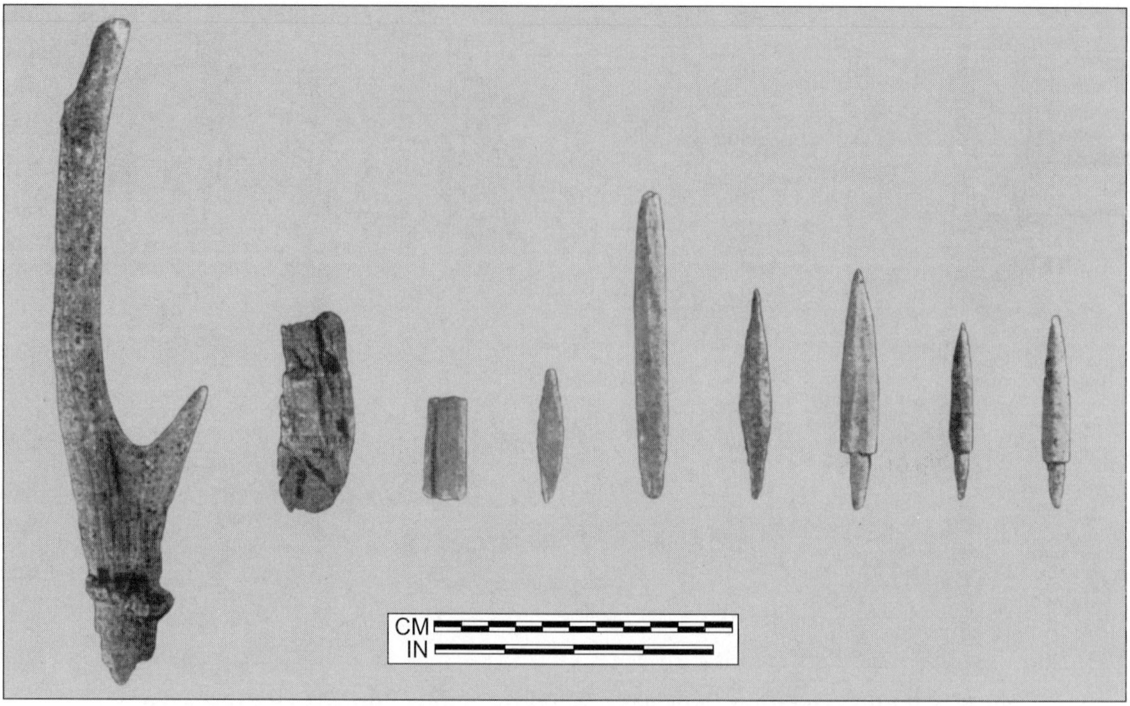

Plate III. Allahpur, different stages of making an arrowhead from antler, (See page-53).

Plate IV. Banavasi, excavations of a brick Chaitya, Satavahana period, (See page-57).

regular pattern it is presumed that the bone structure was revolving on a definite axle.

There are brown encrustations on one of the bone implements which, on testing, were found to be an oxide of iron ($Fe_2 O_3$) –n-H_2O. It was further confirmed by micro-chemical analysis. The brown coloured rings were of the same chemical composition as the grain deposits.

After fabrication, the tools seem to have been polished with the help of smooth stones and finally rubbed with soft skin. Another way of polishing these tools was to use wax or oil.

TYPOLOGY

The bone objects numbering 150 can be divided into the following typess:

A. POINTS

(*a*) *Double ended points*

(i) Sharp point and tapering tang.

(ii) Tang and body similar in form to the extent that they cannot be differentiated. They are generally without polish.

(*b*) *Tanged-points*

(i) Circular point divided from the tang by a flange. The tang and point are well defined and highly polished.

(ii) Long circular point with a small tapering tang.

(*c*) *Long socketed point*

(i) Long circular point with socket behind.

(ii) Elliptical point with socket behind and also having simple incised designs on both the surfaces.

(*d*) *Hollow point with iron filling and tang hollow*

(i) An example of this implement is of particular interest. A thin iron rod is found inserted in this cavity. The blade-body was hollow since the portion of the bone used was either naturally or intentionally made hollow. The iron was used to achieve the required heaviness not only to avoid flying off mid-way but also to make it an effective piercing weapon. In all probability the tang was also of iron; in fact it appears to be an extension of the portion inside the cavity. Big hollow thorns of *babul* tree are used in this fashion in many parts of India.

B. Stilus

(i) Stilus with simple point.

C. Awl

(i) Long tapering awl with a groove near the point.
(ii) Tapering awl with simple point.

The researches done during the last twenty years have revealed a sizable number of bone implements from different excavations at Burzahom, Chirand, Ujjain, Nasik, etc, The working on raw antler is characteristic of Sarai Nahar Rai[9] and Chirand[10], etc. On the basis of these discoveries we may group the bone implements into the following culturai categories :

I Mesolithic (Sarai Nahar Rai)
II Neolithic (Chirand and Burzahom)
III Harappa (Mohenjo-daro, Chanhu-daro, Lothal, etc.)
IV Post-Harappan Chalcolithic Culture (Navdatoli, etc.)
V Painted Grey Ware (Hastinapur and Allahapur)
VI N. B. P. and Post-N. B. P. (Ujjain, Taxila, Kausambi, Nasik. Sonpur, etc.)

The variety of bone arrowheads, awls, etc., from Group I to IV are limited whereas from Group V and VI the tools are more in number and in variety of shapes. They are also found distributed in a much wider area. The objects of the later groups are very well finished and highly polished. The tradition of bone arrowheads, etc.. continued even up to c. A. D. 1000 (Ruper V).

References

1. The site was excavated under the joint direction of Dr. Romila Thapar of

Delhi University and Shri K. N. Dikshit of the National Museum, New Delhi. The countryside was well populated in the past by the hoardes of deers. Even ten years back the number was quite large but due to merciless hunting, they are now more or less extinct from this region.

2. Arrowheads of bone and iron are found mentioned in the *Rigveda* and *Samhitas*. Kautilya (*bk. II. ch. 18*) also mentioned five kinds of arrow-heads made of iron, bone or wood. To smear poison on the tip of the arrowhead was a common practice. See also S. P. Gupta, "Arrowhead-Its technology and History", in *Journal of the Bihar Research Society*, vol. XLVII, January-December, Patna, 1961, pp. 129-42.

3 B. B. Lal, "Excavations at Hastinapura and other Explorations in the Upper Ganga and Sutlej Basins 1950—52," *Ancient India*, nos. 10 & 11, New Delhi, 1955, pp, 13-14. See also *Indian Archaeology 1956-57—A Review*, New Delhi, p. 27. In the excavations at Ujjain, one of the bone arrow-heads was stained with the blood of a bird. A collapsed manufacturing of bone arrow-heads was also noticed (*IAR 57-58* p. 36 and pl. XLIII B). Bone industries were also reported in the past from the N. B. P. and post-N. B. P. levels of Kausambi, Taxila, Nasik and Sonpur.

4. Shri R. K. Pant of the Archaeological Survey of India, Srinagar, is currently working on this problem.

5. S. A. Semenov, *Prehistoric Technology* (London, 1964), p. 145.

6. G. Watt, and P. Brown, *Indian Art Exhibition, Delhi* (Cal., 1903), p. 196.

7. Information from Shri E. Duncan of the National Museum, New Delhi. The author accompanied him to the workshops of ivory, antler, bone, etc.

8. Information from Shri B. N. Tandon, National Museum, New Delhi. The microscopic studies on bone tools were carried out by him.

9. Information from Shri Hem Raj of the Department of Archaeology, Government of Uttar Pradesh, Lucknow. The author had a chance to examine the material in 1970.

10. Information from Dr. B. S. Verma, now of the Arch. Surv. of India.

K. N. Dikshit

EXCAVATIONS OF A BRICK APSIDAL TEMPLE AT BANAVASI, DISTRICT NORTH CANARA

Banavasi is a small town in the Sirsi Taluk of North Kanara District, Mysore State. But in the early centuries of the Christian era, it was a great capital of Karnataka and was ruled by the Satavahanas, Kadambas and Chalukyas. The ancient site comprising a number of mounds covers an area of more than one square mile. Some of the mounds are 15-20 feet in height and contain brick structures. The bricks are large and typically Satavahana in character. Similar bricks were encountered in 1929 on the Satavahana site of Chandravalli, Chitaldrug Distrct, Mysore State.

At the centre of the town is situated the mediaeval temple of Madhukesvara, adjoining the bank of the river Varada. The sanctum sanctorum may be considerably older exhibiting some Kadamba features. The beautiful figure of Madhava now kept in the Sukanasi of the Madhukesvara temple belongs to the Chalukyan period. It has on its *prabhavali* the figures depicting the ten *avatars* of Vishnu. Considerable additions and renovation were carried out under the Kings of Vijayanagara and the Nayaks.

Inscriptions are not lacking at the place. On the four faces of a granite square pillar, was found in box-headed Brahmi a Kadamba inscription, the first of its kind, at Banavasi. It mentions the names of Kakusthavarman, Santivarman and Mrigesavarman of the Kadamba dynasty and refers to what seems to be a victory over the Pallavas for Mrigesavarman. Another Kadamba inscription found at Gudnapur in the vicinity of Banavasi belongs to the period of Ravivarma and mentions the names of the father and grand-father respectively of Mayurasarman, the celebrated founder of the Kadamba dynasty.

A number of coin hoards have been reported from the site. Sri Wodeyar produced, when we visited the place, the lead coins of Chutukulananda and Mulananda and also the well-known potin types of Yajna Sri with the elephant having an uplifted trunk on the obverse. He had even preserved the red polished pottery vase which contained the Yajna Sri coins.

There is a huge brick fortification enclosing the present habitation and most of the temples mentioned above. It is constructed of large-sized bricks measuring 16″ ×

3″ with a rubble foundation. The walls of the defences seem to have undergone repairs twice: once when brick bats were employed in large quantities and a second time when large-sized laterite blocks were used for that purpose. Similar laterite blocks are used even now for construction work.

One of the mounds (BNV I) was partly cut away for earth to construct a road bridge across the Varada river by Public Works Department contractors. The brick walls within the mound had been pulled out. Excavations were carried out here to determine the character of the building. The bricks were large-sized and measured 18″×10″×3″. The section revealed three stumps of brick walls with a platform projecting from it. Digging went down to the natural soil exposing four layers and a pit. The lower portion was much disturbed and on chasing the aps:dal portion of the walls, it was possible to find out the plan of the building. The bricks were laid out in the English bond system, i.e., alternate course of headers and stretchers.

On the whole, the structure turned out to be an apsidal temple with a platform. The local tradition believes that the mound contained a *Chaityagriha* and it may also be recalled that Huan Tsang who is credited to have visited Banavasi in the 7th Century mentioned the existence of a *Chaitya* on the banks of the Varada. Large quantities of floor tiles were found from the probable floor level of the structure indicating that the floor was paved with them. Two architectural pieces of stone belonging to this mound and said to have been found during the ransacking of the mound by the Public Works Department contractors werea *chandrasila* and a door jamb. The structure when completely dug up measured 26×13·5 metres. Perhaps it is one of the largest brick *Chaityas* of the Satavahana period in the whole of south India.

In BNV II layers 5 and 6 represent the habitation of the site in the first half of the first century A. D. since it is these which yielded Russet-coated painted ware and immitation rouletted ware. In layer 5 was also found the remnants of a wall with large-sized Satavahana bricks.

Excavation was continued again during February 1971, and another large brick *Chaitya* (BNV VI) of the Satavahana Period was discovered on the bank adjoining the river. When completely dug up it measured 22·5×12·5 metres. The immitation-rouletted ware and the Russet-coated kaolin painted ware were also found in the layer below the structure. The date of this brick structure is therefore somewhat later than the first Century A.D. (Plate IV)

—M. SESHADRI

EXPLORATIONS OF PREHISTORIC SITES IN DISTRICT BIJAPUR

SOME UNUSUAL TOOL-TYPES FROM ANAGWADI

The site Anagwadi, District Bijapur, Mysore, has provided a very good evidence of Acheulian industry through the excavations carried out by the writer.[1] The Early Stone Age Acheulian industry of Anagwadi consists mainly of varied and numerous forms of handaxes and cleavers, as also other tool-types like choppers, scrapers and discoids. The tool assemblage, besides containing these usual forms, is characterised by the presence of a few peculiar forms showing clear evidence of hafting, notches in anterior portion, beak-shaped points etc.

DESCRIPTION OF THE TOOL-TYPES

The following four categories of tools of unusual forms are described below:

(i) Tools showing evidence of hafting.

(ii) Tools with notches.

(iii) Tools with beak shaped projection.

(iv) Tools with chisel edges.

(i) *Tools showing evidence of hafting*

It was thought by Foote[2] long back that many of the handaxes and cleavers were hafted. Sankalia[3] suggested that many of the pointed handaxes with comparatively heavy butts and cleavers with pointed butt ends (V-shaped) were hafted in wood or bamboo and the former could have served as spear-heads. Instance of handaxes with intentionally made tangs are rather rare. Supekar[4] has reported one such tool having convex working-edge and well-made tang from Hasalpur, Central Narmada basin. In the Anagwadi collection there are three such handaxes with well made tangs thereby showing undoubted evidence of hafting. One of the specimens is described below:

ANGW—125 (Fig. I,4)

An oval shaped handaxe on flake. Deep flake scars at butt end intentionally made to produce tang. Pebble cortex retained in central and butt portion. Tip end portion carefully worked. Shallow flake scars, prominent in general. Tip rounded.

Cross-section: asymmetrical biconvex. Brown quartzite. (110 × 73 × 35mm).[5]

(ii) *Tools with Notches*

Handaxes with notches, producing waist on the lateral sides, are of rare occurrence in the Early Stone Age industries in India. Notched Middle Acheulian ovates and Early Levallois flakes have been reported from Warsash, Hampshire (England), and Montieres (France) respectively. Specimens resembling these forms of handaxes were found in the Acheulian industry of Anagwadi. It appears that two prominent notches were meant for the purpose of hafting and butt end with edge all around as functional part of the tool either for cutting or chopping purposes. There are five specimens of this type in the collection and one of them is described below:

ANGW—73 (Fig I,5)

An elongated pear shaped handaxe on flake. Both under as well as upper sides fully worked. Shallow flake scars prominent. Numerous step flakes on both sides. Deliberately made notches in the anterior portion along lateral sides. Tip rounded. Cross-section: asymmetrical biconvex. Pink quartzite. (162 × 90 × 5Cmm)

(iii) *Tools with Beak shaped Projection*

In this category of tool-types a deep flake has been removed at the tip portion on one of the lateral sides of the tool so that the tool has beak like appearance. The presence of this prominent characteristic notch suggests that tools probably served as spoke-shaves for the shaping of wooden spears and also were useful for scraping flesh from long bones. There are three specimens of this category in the collection :

(a) Handaxe with beak Shaped Projection

This specimen was collected at a site Yedhalli situated 4 kms. downstream of Anagwadi.

YDHL—2 (Fig. I, 1)

A handaxe with beak shaped projection. Made on pebble. Shallow flake scars, prominent on both surfaces. A large patch of pebble cortex in the center. Deep concavity at the anterior portion. Cross-section: biconvex. Brown quartzite. (105 × 60 × 35mm).

(b) Beak Shaped Tool on Block

ANGW—258 (Fig. I, 2)

A specimen with prominent beak shaped projection. Made on rectangular natural block. Working restricted only along one face of the block. Other face completely unworked. Shallow flake scars prominent. Deep notch at tip portion. Part of the portion near tip end made flat for proper grip. Grey quartzite (105x51x35mm).

(c) Rostrocarinate tool types

There are four specimens of rostrocarinate type in the collection and these are similar to one described by C. van Riet Lowe [7]. In these, an oval shaped pebble is longitudinally split into two halves. The flat plain surface obtained by splitting is not further worked while high backed upper surface is completely or partly flaked in such a way as to get a central ridge or keel. At the tip end beak shaped point is produced by making a deep notch.

ANGW—77 (Fig. I, 3)

A handaxe with rostrocarinate form. Underside clean and flat excepting a few flake scars along margins. Deep flake scar at tip portion. Upper side highly backed; partly worked and characterised by median ridge. Pebble cortex retained over large area. Cross-section: triangular. Grey quartzite (120×70×40mm).

(iv) *Tools with Chisel Edges*
There are two specimens in the collection which are characterised by short chisel edges at the tip portion. Both these specimens can be grouped in the 'chopper' class of tool-types. The flaking on these tools is regulated in such a way that short chisel working edge is produced.

(a) ANGW—(Fig. I, 7)

A specimen with short chisel end on round based pebble. Butt end unworked. Flaking confined mainly to anterior portion on both sides. Chisel edge produced by vertical flaking at tip portion. Pink quartzite. (120×110×65mm).

(b) ANGW—75 (Fig. I, 6)

A specimen with short chisel end made on natural block. Shallow flake scars

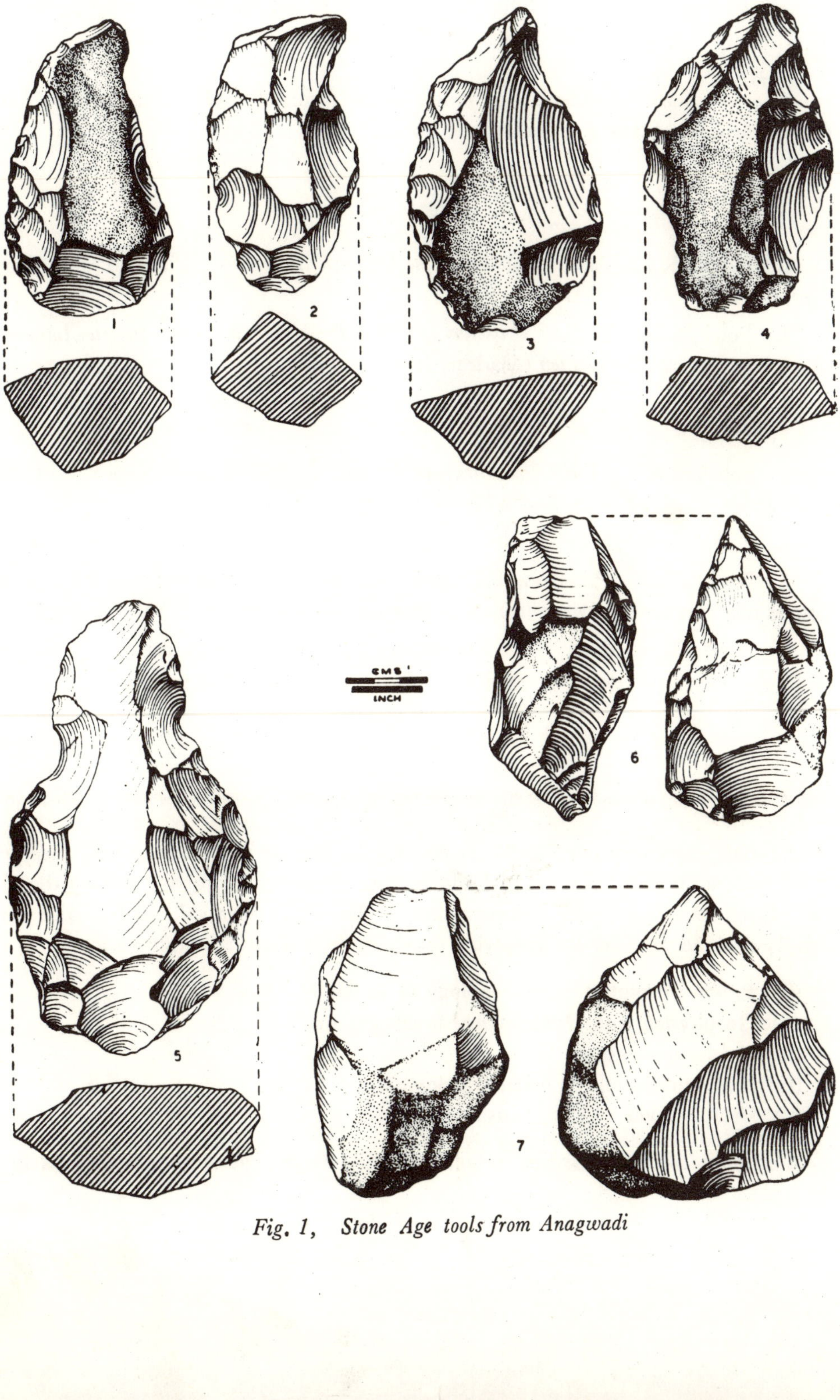

Fig. 1, Stone Age tools from Anagwadi

prominent all over the surface. Short and sharp chisel edge produced at tip portion by vertical flaking. Butt end fully worked. Pink quartzite. (115×70×52mm).

The presence of the above mentioned unique forms of tools indicates the advance nature of the Early Stone Age industry in India.

References

1. Pappu, R.S., *Pleistocene Studies in the Upper Krishna Basin,* Ph. D. Thesis, Poona University (1966). Unpublished.

2. Foote, R.B., *The Foote Collection of Indian Pre-historic and Proto-historic Antiquities, Notes on their Ages and Distribution* (Madras, 1916), p. 173.

3. Sankalia, H.D., *Stone Age Tools—Their Techniques, Names and Probable Functions* (Poona, 1964), p. 92.

4. Supekar, S.G., *Pleistocene Stratigraphy and Prehistoric Archaeology of the Central Narmada Basin*, Ph. D. Thesis, Poona University (1968). Unpublished.

5. The measurements are given in millimeters in length, breadth and thickness.

6. Burkitt, M.C., Paterson, T.T., and Mogridge, G. J , "The Lower Palaeolithic Industries near Warsash", *Proceedings of the Prehistoric Society*, vol. V (1939), pp. 39-47

7. Lowe, C. van Riet, "The Pleistocene Geology and Pre-history of Uganda", Pt.II, Pre-history, *Geological Survey of Uganda Memoir*, no. VI (1952) p. 30.

R. S. Pappu

A 5-day symposium on "Radiocarbon Applications in Archaeology and Geophysics" will be held at the Institute of Fundamental Research, Bombay, during the first half of March 1972 under the Secretaryship of Dr. D. P. Agrawal. It has also been tentatively decided to cover the following topics in the various scientific sessions:

(i) Pre-and Protohistoric chronology in India.
(ii) Geophysical and Hydrological investigations.
(iii) Pleistocene studies.
(iv) Synthetic models on archaeological data.
(v) Decipherment of the Indus script.

A number of distinguished scholars from foreign countries are also likely to attend.

BOOK REVIEWS

THE INDIAN CIVILISATION : THE FORMATIVE PERIOD
(INDIAN INSTITUTE OF ADVANCED STUDY, SIMLA, 1968) PRICE: Rs. 20.

By S. C. Malik

For years there was no sequel to Subbarao's book, *The Personality of India.* That was a brave and pioneering work, an attempt to understand archaeological data Both before him and afterwards, there have come out a number of important books on Indian archaeology but most of them have 'described' the archaeological evidence rather than interpreting it. It is therefore gratifying to note that a thought-provoking book on interpretative archaeology has finally come out, and that too from the pen of a worthy student of the late Subbarao. Malik's book brings in some fresh air into the world of now stale archaeological reports.

Malik has tried to interpret and understand the phenomenon of the Harappa culture, by way of illustration of the approach he wants to use. He has not only tried to theorise on the Harappa culture, but also to explain the personality of India and its so-called changelessness. In doing this he lands himself in trouble.

In trying to prove the changelessness of India he conceives of trade-routes of the hunting-gathering stage which were used later on by the urban centres. Now regular trade and its routes are concomitants of civilisation; they had no function in the food gathering early Stone Ages. Then he quotes the changelessness of the Harappan script. Who has studied the changes, if any, stratigraphically. S. R. Rao holds that the script has developed. One knows however that the Brahmi script was a dynamic and changing script.

There is something lacking in the marshalling of the archaeological data or its mature appreciation. For example, he denies the existence of lavatories in the Harappan times; his assumption that the Harappa culture developed out of the Pre-Harappan cultures. Tracing this development has so far been an elusive problem for the archaeologists but the author makes a bland but far-reaching statement without bothering to prove it.

There are many assumptions of the author which are put across as proven facts, e.g., there was no legal coercion in the Harappa culture.

In his preoccupation with the changelessness he merges the Bronze Age revolution of the Harappa cultures, that started in the 24th century B.C., into the Iron Age one in the Doab which cannot be placed earlier than the 6th century B. C. Similarly he says that there were inter-related settlements all over India in the mid-IInd millennium B. C. Now where is the evidence for all this ?

In his method all generalisations emerge from the theories of the new American anthropologists, without due regard for Indian data. He seems to have made them inexorable laws. He reminds one of Dange's work (*India: from Primitive Communism to Slavery*) in which he quotes Marxist scriptures and then looks for their Indian parallels.

Proper theorising requires a full and digested knowledge of the archaeological data. He neither takes into account the ecological zones nor the time factors involved. The second urban revolution of the Doab was a direct product of the Iron Age and had hardly anything to do with the Harappa Culture. Of course, in the later day Hindu culture and ethos a number of cultures contributed through the millennia, a major source being the Harappa Culture.

The author has not cared to mention the far-reaching technological advances which help us build socio-economic patterns from the mute artifacts. Nor the use of randomised data sampling, statistical analysis and modelling techniques to make the archaeology a social science. How archaeological research has to be 'designed' for testing specific hypothesis needed to be told.

Instead of quoting extensively from American anthropologists' theories only, he was expected to give some of the methodologies of New Archaeology. For valid reconstructions of the prehistoric Indian society, one cannot just extrapolate from theories, as if they were some absolute laws. S. P. Gupta in his recent book on the Disposal of the Dead and Physical Types in Ancient India has discussed this point at length and then pertinently remarked that the Social Laws are not to be equated with the Laws of Nature; in fact the use of the term 'Laws' in the context of Social Science is not correct. One has to use a thousand ingenious ways to learn about the extinct societies. For example, mapping of distribution of Pollen in different rooms led to the determination of various room functions, and groupings of activities within the community. Or the use of systems analysis in Oxaco valley for studying the change from nomadic to sedentary life style and beginnings of social stratification. Or the various inter-disciplinary methods being used to reconstruct the Pueblo societies.

Reconstruction of extinct communities is much more difficult than appears from Malik's facile theoretical extrapolations. It requires the arsenal of tools and techniques used by New Archaeology and painstaking work. Data collection using the new multidisciplinary tools will alone lead to objective inferences about the past Indian societies. One hopes that in the revised edition of the book an attempt will be made to create a multidimensional awareness of the archaeological problems.

There are two vital roles his book could play: (i) to shake the Indian archaeologists from their 'descriptive' stupor; and (ii) to show a constructive way of synthesising the archaeological data. In the first aim, the book succeeds pre-eminently. The second purpose requires a more sustained work in depth.

A reviewer's task is very easy. He can extol a work or shatter it to pieces—without ever producing a constructive piece himself. Whatever criticism is offered here is meant as an appeal not only to improve but to drastically transform the revised editions. The reviewer has great expectations from the young and creative anthropologist that Dr. Malik is. We are all thankful to him for shaking us out of our stupor; but now he has to work harder to show us the proper way.

D. P. Agrawal

A BIBLIOGRAPHY ON INDIAN MEGALITHS

(STATE DEPARTMENT OF ARCHAEOLOGY, GOVERNMENT OE TAMILNADU, 1971)
XI+184 PP. AND 18 FIGURES, PRICE RS. 12.50

By K. S. Ramachandran

There has been an almost-total absence of bibliographical material pertaining to Indian archaeological studies. This lack of essential research-tool sadly reflects the state of archaeological studies in our country, resulting thereby in a lop-sided approach to the subjects. That is so since, more otten than not, the latest publications are not easily available to the research workers engaged in different areas of study. Ramachandran's *Bibliography* seeks to, and goes a long way to fulfill this need, particularly of those scholars who have no direct access to the literature on the subject and some of which is already out of print and inaccessible.

Originally serialized in the *Quarterly Journal of the Mythic Society* (Vols. LII, nos. 1-4, LIII, nos. 3 & 4, and LIV, nos. 1 & 2, published between the years 1961-1963), this *Bibliography* has been brought up to date by Ramachandran (till 1970) and incorporates almost all the relevant literature on Indian megaliths. As it is, the task of listing the articles in itself is quite considerable and the compiler has added to the utility of the work by not merely alphabetically listing the various entries, but has also provided brief synopsis for each entry. Besides, an index of the megalithic types and sites in India and a general index have also been added to provide the reader with ready-reference. A glossary of terms and a chart equating the terminology and nomenclature used by various workers in the field with that used by the pioneer in the field, V.D. Krishnaswami, has also been given. Ramachandran has thus succeeded in giving an almost encyclopaedic character to his *Bibliography*, exaggerated though it may sound to those unused to such efforts. To those unacquainted with the basic types and the areas of their distribution, a map and illustrations of the megaliths would prove particularly useful.

As has been pointed by B. K. Thapar in his Introduction to the *Bibliography*, interest in the study of Indian megaliths really began with the publication of James Fergusson's classic work *Rude Stone Monuments in All Countries: Their Ages and Uses*, even though the megalithic tombs of Malabar had been excavated by Babington as early as in 1823. Notwithstanding the many discoveries and the attempts at various academic levels to collate the ever-increasing data, much remained to be done till V.D. Krishnaswami took up the study of the subject and came out with the classification of the megalithic types of south India, which was published in *Ancient India*, no. 5, 1949. However, the problems connected with their chronology, cultural association, etc., continued to remain an enigma and led to much controversy verging on polemic at times. Even with regard to the nomenclature of the various megalithic types, there seems to be no unanimity. Ramachandran's chart equating the terminology and nomenclature evolved by the various scholars with that of Krishnaswmi and the glossary of terms would be of great help to the beginners and to those who are not acquainted with the material and are likely to misunderstand the facts for this lack of standardized nomenclature.

With the latest discoveries of the megalithic remains in the areas outside the peninsular parts of India which have extended the boundaries of the megalithic remains to the northern-most parts of India, the subject has assumed still greater importance. This *Bibliography* should serve as an introduction to those who desire to delve into this fascinating, yet a vexed, problem. To those who are already engaged in this study, this *Bibliography* would be of permanent value.

Ramachandran has put in much labour in the preparation of the work. In the 369 entries, he has included almost all the material pertaining to the megalithic remains and theoretical studies thereof dealing with the various aspects of the megaliths in India. Unfortunately not much care seems to have been taken at the time of its printing and almost every page abounds in printing mistakes. The compiler could also have systematized the annotation by adopting a standard pattern; this, however, does not detract the quality or lessen the importance of the work. It is hoped that this shortcoming would be taken care of in the next edition and the co-ordinates of the sites would also be given.

B. M. Pande

THE COPPER-BRONZE AGE IN INDIA

(MUNSHIRAM MANOHARLAL, DELHI, 1971); PAGES 270. PRICE RS. 55

by D. P. Agrawal

This book presents a comprehensive survey of the protohistoric period in India based on the archaeological, technological and ecological data set in a logically argued chronological framework, which is based on the archaeological evidence as well as on a critical assessment of the C^{14} dates of which the author is a leading exponent in India. The book deals with the evidence on the copper-technology of the different cultures and assesses the role of the interaction of technology and the prevailing ecology in the genesis and growth of various protohistoric cultures. The book provides an authoritative summary of the evidence on metal-technology and chronology of the protohistoric cultures, and succinctly deals with the ecological background of not only the Indus Valley Civilization and its wide ramifications both in time and space but also of the early cultures of the Doab,and of Central and Western India. The evaluation of Raikes' theories of the impounding of the Indus is indeed stimulating. The book offers the first serious attempt at a multi-disciplinary approach for the reconstruction of Indian protohistory.

It may, however, be pointed out that at places the text has become a bit too terse. The author has tried to cover a vast gamut in a short book of this type; he should have elaborated the data in greater details. The section on ecology appears weaker than others, perhaps due to the paucity of relevant data. The system of reference, though novel and space-saving, seems a little cumbersome. For the wealth of latest references on a number of relevant topics, however, the book is exceptionally rich and rewarding.

The printing and get up of the book are excellent. The price of the book, however, is a little high for the pocket of the student and the 'private' scholar.

Krishna Deva

READINGS IN INDIAN ARCHAEOLOGY

Abstract from "The Indus Valley Culture (Seen in the context of Post-Glacial climate and Ecological studies in North-West India)" by Gurdip Singh of the Deptt. of Biogeography and Geomorphology, Research School of Pacific Studies, Australian National University, Canberra, published in *Archaeology and Physical Anthropology in Oceania*, vol. VI, No. 2, July, 1971 pp. 177-189.

One of the most debated of the issues concerning the Indus people in recent years has been regarding the postulated occurrence of higher rainfall conditions during the period they are known to have flourished in north-west India. Ever since Stein (1931), on the basis of the occurrence of "gabar bands" (dam-like structures constructed artificially by prehistoric man), suggested the possibility of a significant decline in rainfall of Baluchistan since prehistoric times resulting from climatic change, other authors have produced additional evidence, in one form or another, to support the hypothesis (Marshall 1931; Vats, 1940; Wheeler, 1968; Chowdhury and Ghosh, 1951). Deductions on the nature of climate during Harappan times have so far, however, rested on indirect evidence provided by human artifacts, such as sculptures, drawings and engravings of animals and plants on potsherds and steatite seals, burnt bricks, animal bones, wood and charcoal remains, flooding horizons and the occurrence of "gabar bands". In recent years, the testimony to higher rainfall argued for each of these lines of evidence has been questioned by some authors (Raikes, 1964, 1965*a*, 1965*b*; Raikes and Dyson, 1961; Dales, 1966). Without going into details either for or against the issue at this stage, it may suffice to say that sufficient weight had been attached to the counter-arguments for Dales (1966, p. 131) to say: "Convincing evidence, collected from both archaeological and natural science investigations, refutes the popular theories of appreciable climatic change in the South Asian area during the past four to five thousand years (Raikes, 1965*a*; Raikes and Dyson, (1961). Climate has thus been practically eliminated as a major factor in the environmental fortunes of the Harappan civilization."

The interests of the present author, who is primarily a plant palaeoecologist, do not rest directly in the line of archaeology. Recently, however, a series of new evidence has emerged from pollen-analytical studies of salt-lake deposits carried out by the author in an area centring on the Rajasthan desert in north-west India, which reflect closely on the nature of climate of the period of the Indus Valley culture and has largely prompted the present contribution (Singh, 1970). Besides the post-glacial climatic sequence, the studies have also brought out evidence suggesting the possibility of early primitive agriculture in north-west India, antedating the Harappan culture by about five thousand years.

The present contribution is an attempt to open the question of the nature of climate governing the Indus culture once again and to consider the rise and fall of this culture in a palaeoecological context. with special reference to the possibility of a gradual evolution of the art of agriculture in north-west India since early postglacial times.

THE AREA INVESTIGATED

The area covered by the present investigations is broadly comprised of the State of Rajasthan (20°3′ N.–30° 12′ N. latitudes and 69° 30′ E.–78° 17′ E. longitudes), and some bordering areas in the adjoining States of the Punjab, Haryana and western Uttar Pradesh, in noth-west India. The investigations comprising studies on the late-Quaternary history were confined to the Rajasthan territory, whereas the work on surface samples for determining basic criteria for the interpretation of pollen diagrams was extended to the other provinces.

STRATIGRAPHICAL, PALAEOECOLOGICAL, AND CULTURAL CONSIDERATIONS

The known time range of the Indus culture, which is about five hundred years, is only a small fraction of the Holocene period. While it would be quite futile to dwell in detail on the findings pertaining to the entire post-glacial period, it is necessary to have a long-range perspective of the climatic sequence for a consideration of the development of the late-Holocene cultures, including the Harappan culture, in their natural settings. It is therefore proposed to present an outline of post-glacial environmental history preceding the Indus Valley culture, together with some of the basic evidence, and to discuss the same in the light of the known cultural history.

The environmental sequence which is built up here from the vegetational history deduced from pollen analysis has been grouped into six phases of which all but phase I belong to the Holocene period. Phase I, which is primarily inferred from the general stratigraphy of the salt-lake basins, is pre–Holocene. Phases III, IV and VI are further suhdivided into subphase IIIa, IIIb, IVa, IVb, IVc, VIa and VIb, following the zonation of the pollen diagrams. The pollen record comes wholly from the Holocene. as fossil pollen is not preserved in the pre-Holocene sandy material. The post-glacial pollen sequences from the sites investigateda re divisible into five zones termed A, B, C, D and E, of which zones B, C and E are subdivided into sub-zones B_1, B_2, C_1, C_2, C_3, E_1, and E_2. The original pollen diagrams, together with their detailed descriptions, will be published elsewhere. In the present discussion only phases I, II, III and a part of phase IV, which are relevant to the Indus Valley culture, are considered.

Phase I : Before 8000 B.C.

The evidence for phase I comes mainly from the stratigraphy of the salt-lake basins. The earliest lake sediments, which date from early Holocene times at all the sites, are underlain by a thick bed of loosely packed, wind-borne sand. In each case the sand is seen to extend horizontally to meet the sand dunes (which are now stabilized) encircling the individual salt-lake basins. This suggests that the basins were probably formed during pre-Holocene times by the damming of ancient valleys by wind-borne sand, at a time when the sand dunes were still active. While the beginning of this phase of severe, pre-Holocene aridity is uncertain, there is evidence that the phase ended with an increase in rainfall at about the beginning of the Holocene period. This is shown by two radiocarbon assays obtained separately from Sambhara (9253±130 B.P., TF–887) and Lunkaransar (9260±115 B.P., WIS–405), from levels about 30–40 cm. above the sand/clay boundaries at the two sites. From these results a date for the infilling of the lake basins can be extrapolated of around 10,000 B.P.

There is practically nothing known of the human cultures occupying north-west India during this phase. At present there appears to be a somewhat abrupt break between the largely Upper Pleistocene Middle Stone Age cultures and the exclusively post-glacial microlithic Late Stone Age cultures in north west India. This is quite unlike the situation prevailing in southern India, where the change from Middle to Late Stone Age, that is to say from the flake to the microlithic tradition, appears to have been a process of continuous development rather than of sudden change (Allchin and Allchin, 1968, p. 78). Whether the hiatus between the Middle Stone Age and the Late Stone Age cultures in north-west India was in some manner influenced by the severe aridity prevailing during pre-Holocene times is not certain. From the present evidence it would, however, appear that the central core of north-west India was affected by severe aridity and that the territory would have been unsuitable for habitation for a long time during at least the later part of the last glacial.

Phase II : Pollen zone A : 8000 B.C.-c. 7500 B.C.

This phase starts with the first sedimentation of freshwater lacustrine deposits in the lake basins, a development that appears to have occurred at about the beginning of the Holocene period around 10,000 B.P. The lake sediments consist of laminated clays and contain a fair amount of fossil pollen at all the sites, thus allowing the reconstruction of the vegetational history of the post-glacial period.

The vegetation as deduced from the pollen record in phase II, represented by pollen zone A, is comprised of high values for sedges and grasses and low values for halopytes denoted by Chenopodiaceae/Amaranthaceae. *Artemisia*, which now grows abundantly under a higher rainfall regime (above 50 cm. average annual rainfall) mostly in the Himalayan foothill plains and which is at present rarely seen in the Rajasthan desert, appears to have flourished in large numbers during this phase in both the contemporary Arid and the Semi-Arid belts. Mesophytic plants such as *Mimosa rubicaulis* and *Oldenlandia*, which now grow mostly east of the Aravalli Range and upcountry in Punjab and Haryana, are indicated as having occupied the Semi-Arid belt in western Rajasthan. There is little desert vegetation represented in the Semi-Arid belt in this phase : small quantities of *Ephedra* pollen, which is notorious for being wind-transported over long distances (Maher, 1964), is, however, seen regularly; a few grains of *Maytenus*, a desert plant species, make their appearance in the later part of the sequence in this phase. As there is no further intercalation of sand layers in the lake sediments, it is suggested that the sand dunes had started to stabilize. That the rainfall was considerably more than that of the present day, with freshwater conditions prevailing in the lake basins, is apparently testified by the presence, in both the Arid and the Semi-Arid belts, of *Typha angustata*, a freshwater aquatic species no longer seen in the Rajasthan desert beyond the 50 cm. isohyetal line. The present evidence would thus indicate that there was an excess of at least 25 cm. (10 in.) of precipitation over the present in the Arid belt in phase II.

Phase II corresponds in time to the pre-Boreal period in Europe, when temperatures are known to have started rising throughout the world, including north-west India, following the final recession of the last glacial (von Post, 1946; Godwin, 1956; Iversen, 1954; Singh, 1963). In the Rajasthan desert, as is seen above, the climatic change is suggested to have taken the form of an increase in rainfall.

The state of human cultures occupying the Rajasthan desert during this phase is largely a matter of conjecture, as work on Late Stone Age microlithic cultures in India is still in its infancy. Nevertheless, the climatic conditions of the Rajasthan area, as inferred above, appear to have been favourable enough to support freshwater bodies and perennial river courses, which in turn can be expected to have supported animal and human populations.

Phase III : Pollen zone B : c. 7500 B.C.-c. 3000 B.C.

The initial rise in precipitation in phase II appears to have given way to a slight lowering of rainfall around 7500 B.C., which was, however, not severe enough substantially to alter the overall ecological patterns already established during the earlier phase. While the sedges decline, the halophytic vegetation, represented by Chenopodiaceae/Amaranthaceae, starts a gradual rise. Desert shrubs, such as *Maytenus* and *Capparis*, begin to occur more regularly in the Semi-Arid belt. The freshwater aquatic vegetation, consisting of *Typha angustata*, *T. latifolia* and *Potamogeton*, was apparently not affected, suggesting the continuation of freshwater environments in the lake basins. Mesophytic plant species *Artemisia*, *Oldenlandia* and *Mimosa rubicaulis* are also suggested to have continued flourishing in the Semi-Arid belt, and all except *Mimosa rubicaulis* occurred, to a lesser degree, in the Arid belt.

Phase III, which is represented by pollen zone B and ranges between *c*. 7500 B.C. and *c*. 3000 B.C., can be broadly equated chronologically with the combined Boreal and Atlantic periods of Europe (Godwin, 1960). Its lower limit is determined by two radiocarbon analyses mentioned earlier from Sambhar (9250±130 B.P., TF–887) and Lunkaransar (9260±115 B.P., WIS–405), dating the boundary between pollen zones A and B to about 7500 B.C. at both sites.

Early Agriculture : The late Stone Age microlithic culture (or cultures) which preceded the Neolithic-Chalcolithic cultures in north-west India and is most likely to have been dominant in the Rajasthan area, unfortunately remains undated for most of the part. At a few places where the remains of the culture have been found in stratigraphical context, it tends to overlap the known Neolithic-Chalcolithic cultures in its upper levels, whereas its early history remains almost unfathomed. The earliest radiocarbon dated horizons go back to approximately 5500 B.C., in the rock shelters excavated at Adamgarh hill in the Narbada valley (Allchin *et al*, 1968). These sites, together with another microlithic site at Langhnaj, in Gujarat, show evidence of contemporaneity for a considerable period with Neolithic or later settlements in adjacent regions (Allchin *et al*, *loc. cit.*). Speaking of Langhnaj, Joshi (1963, p. 3) remarks that "on the basis of this site, it may be said that this phase is characterized by communities which have a mixed economy and might be practising some sort of primitive agriculture along with hunting and fishing, domestication of animals to some extent burying their dead and having a slightly more settled pattern of life than the wandering folks".

In the salt-lake profiles from western Rajasthan one witnesses an extraordinary rise in carbonized vegetable remains (mostly wood fragments) in the sediments at about the beginning of phase III (pollen zone B) at all the sites. The phenomenon cannot be explained in terms of natural causes as the enhanced rate of the occurrence is maintained in layer after layer of the lake sediment, starting with phase III. It can be strongly argued that the increase in the burnt remains resulted from the introduction of the practice of scrub burning at the hands of early man, for this alone can explain the synchronous rise in their occurrence in the lake profiles of sites separated by hundreds of kilometres. It is seen that the practice of scrub burning as attested by the above evidence remained at a high level in phases III and IV (pollen zones B and C) and then dwindled away in phases V and VI (pollen zones D and E). It is of considerable interest to note that Cerealia-type pollen (grass pollen more than 40μ; size range $40–50\mu$) also starts occurring in the lake sediments early in phase III (pollen zone B) and continues to appear intermittently throughout phases III and IV at all the sites in close harmony with the enhanced occurrence of carbonized remain The evidence of scrub burning, together with the first occurrence of Cerealia-type pollen in the lake profiles, is dated at 9260 ± 115 B.P. (WIS–405) at Lunkaransar in the extreme west and at 8300 ± 135 B.P. (TF–738) at Sambhar in the extreme east. The close correlation between the occurrence of Cerealia-type pollen on one hand and the evidence of scrub burning on the other raises the obvious question as to whether some sort of primitive cereal agriculture was introduced into the area as far back as 7500 B.C.

Before proceeding any further one may, however, ask whether the Cerealia-type of pollen seen in the salt-lake profiles from Rajasthan does in fact represent cereal pollen. In this regard studies of present-day pollen spectra from 114 samples coming from 64 different sites spread all over north-west India have demonstrated that cereal pollen, mainly because of its large size, is not carried a great distance from its mother source, so that the pollen type is not seen in areas which are free of cereal cultivation. Some wild grasses can indeed be expected to contribute large-sized pollen similar to the Cerealia-type, but the introduction of such wild grasses through purely natural means over an axis of 200 kilometres (separating Lunkaransar from Sambhar) during the same time interval at the beginning of phase III and in conjunction with the first introduction of scrub burning in the territory, seems rather far-fetched. On the other hand, it would appear from the evidence that man had already started interfering with the natural vegetation in western Rajasthan at the beginning of phase III and it is not unreasonable to believe, therefore, that the burning of scrub was probably involved in the practice of some form of primitive cereal agriculture, the like of which was still prevalent with several tribal communities until quite recently in Rajasthan. It goes without saying, however, that the present evidence suggesting an exceptionally early start for cereal agriculture in north-west India needs to be supported with material evidence from excavations at the numerous microlithic settlements found scattered all over the Rajasthan desert, and outside.

Phase IV : Pollen zone C. c. 3000 B.C.–1000 B.C.

At the beginning of this phase, about 3000 B.C., the climate seems to have taken a sudden change to wetter conditions. The period of maximum wetness, however, appears to have lasted only up to about 1800 B.C. Thereafter, the colimate shows a small-scale oscillation to drier conditions between *c.* 1800 B.C. and *c.* 1500 B.C., followed by a slight reversal to a relatively weak wetter interval, lasting up to about 1000 B.C. This period of change is considered as phase IV, which is subdivided into subphases IVa, IVb and IVc, denoting the above threefold oscillation of climate during the mid-post-glacial. Of the three subphases, only subphases IVa and IVb are relevant to the present discussion.

(i) *Subphase IVa : Pollen subzone* C_1 *: c. 3000 B.C.–c. 1800 B.C.* The beginuing of subphase IVa, which is marked by the boundary between pollen zones B and C, is dated around 3000 B.C. from two radiocarbon analyses, 5060±70 (WIS–387) and 5420±70 (WIS–386) from above and below the zonal boundary respectively at Lunkaransar. At Sambhar the date for the same boundary is extrapolated to 3000 B.C. from two radiocarbon determinations, 4665±115 and 4510±110 (TF–739 and TF–884), from about the middle of subhase IVa (subzone C_1).

Palaeoecologically, the subphase starts with a sudden rise in the frequencies of sedges and those of tree and shrub vegetation. The latter rise for the first time in the post-glacial sequence, at all the sites. The trees and shrubs mainly consist of *Syzigium cuminii*, *Mimosa rubicaulis*, *Acacia* sp. *Prosopis cineraria*, *Capparis* sp. and *Tamarix* sp. in the Semi-Arid belt, and of *Calligonum polygonoides*, *Zizyphus* sp., *Prosopis cineraria*, *Maytenus* sp. and *Syzigium cuminii* in the Arid belt. The sedges reach their maximum frequencies more than 500% of all other land-plant pollen in the Semi-Arid belt and are almost as prominently represented in the Arid belt. The present evidence would indicate that *Syzigium cuminii*, a mesophytic tree now growing naturally in India in areas having in excess of 85 cm. (35 in.) average annual rainfally (Troup, 1921), enjoyed a luxuriant growth in the Semi-Arid belt and that it even penetrated the western extreme of Rajasthan, as far as Lunkaransar in the Arid belt. Similarly. *Mimosa rubicaulis*, a mesophytic shrub mentioned earlier in phases II and III, rises to its highest frequencies in the Semi-Arid belt in subphase IVa. *Typha angustata* continues to grow in both the Arid and the Semi-Arid belts as before. The above palaeoecological picture of subphase IVa goes to suggest that relative precipitation over the Rajasthan desert had risen considerably and that the annual average rainfall may have been in excess by at least 50 cm. (20 in.) of the present-day rainfall in the Arid belt. In the light of all this evidence the doubts expressed earlier with respect to a relatively higher rainfall in north-west India during Harappan times (Raikes, 1964*a*, 1965, 1965*b*; Raikes and Dyson, 1961; Dales, 1966) can perhaps now be set aside.

Pollen of Cerealia type, of the same size range as seen in the earlier phase, continues to be met with at all the sites in subphase IVa, without any recognizable hiatus. At the same time evidence for scrub burning in the form of carbonized remains also continues into this subphase.

(ii) *Expansion of Neolithic-Chalcolithic Cultures.* It is of profound interst to note that subphase IVa, in terms of chronology, sees the rise of the pre-Harappan and later on, of the Harappan culture throughout north-west India. It is generally agreed that in the plains of Sind, the Punjab and northern Rajasthan, around the end of the fourth or the beginning of the third millennium B.C., the major expansion of the Neolithic-Chalcolithic way of life took place (Allchin and Allchin, 1968, p. 112). The earliest radiocarbon evidence so far available is the date of pre-Harappan settlement at Kot Diji, placed at 2605 ± 145 B.C. The testimony of Cerealia-type pollen for the existence of cereal agriculture in the latter half of subphase IVa cannot be doubted as the Harappan people are definitely known to have practised cereal cultivation. The question is, however, relevant when the pollen is encountered in earlier horizons.

Here it may be of interest to point out that Cerealia-typo poollen of the tame size range is encountered in good numbers (58% of total land-plant pollen) in the pre-Harappan levels of the Indus Valley site at Kalibangan, excavated by the Archaeological Survey of India. This, together with the unbroken record of Cerealia-type pollen in the pollen profiles and the evidence of forest burning from three different sites, would lead one to believe that the practice of cereal cultivation perhaps does not start with the Indus Valley culture after all but that the practice had existed in the region for a long time, indeed, as has been suggested, from the beginning of phase III. It can in fact be argued that the significant increase in rainfall at the beginning of the third millennium B.C., attested by the palaeoecological evidence, played an important part in the sudden expansion of the Neolithic-Chalcolithic cultures in north-west India, ultimately leading to the prosperity of the Indus culture.

(iii) *Subphase IVb : Pollen subzone* C_2 *: c. 1800 B.C.–c. 1500 B.C.,* The end of subphase IVa and the beginning of subhase IVb can be dated around 1800 B.C. by extrapolation from two Rdiocarbon determinations mentioned earlier (TF–739 and TF–883), from subphase IVa at Sambhar. For subphase IVb the palaeoecological evidence points to a short dry period. The sedges undergo a sudden decline. All the mesophytic plant species found in subphase IVa, such as *Syzigium cuminii, Mimosa rubicaulis* and the freshwater aquatic species, disappear for good from the pollen sequence. At Lunkaransar, in the Arid belt, the horizontal stratification of laminated clays breaks down and pollen is no longer preserved in the sediment, both factors indicating that the lake had started drying out. In the Semi-Arid belt, with the disappearance of freshwater aquatic vegetation, it would appear that the lakes had started turning saline. Indeed there is some rise in the frequencies of halophytic plant species at Sambhar. *All this goes to indicate that a dry period of some intensity had set in about 1800 B.C. It is a rare coincidence that the Harapan culture is known to have started declining around 1750 B.C.* (Agrawal *et al.*, 1964). The archaeological evidence has been interpreted to suggest that the Harappan culture met with a sudden end. The same evidence, however, also indicates that a general decline had already set in much before the final blow (Wheeler, 1968, p. 127), which some believe to have been struck by the Aryan invaders (Wheeler, *loc. cit.*; Allchin, *et al* 1968, pp. 144–156). *The present evidence would suggest that the onset of aridity in the region around 1800 B. C. probably resulted in the weakening of the Harappan culture in the arid and semi-arid parts of north-west India but that the peripheral to the same degree.* The extinction of the Indus culture may have been initiated through gradual decline as a result of climatic change, but the process may yet have been completed by successive invasions from the north-west by the Aryans.*

References

Agrawal, D. P., *et al* (1964): "Radiocarbon Dates of Archaeological samples", *Current Science*, Vol. 33 (9). p. 266.

Allchin, B., *et al* (1968) : *The Birth of Indian Civilization*, Pelican Books.

Chowdhury, K. A., *et al* (1951) : "Plant Remains from Harappa", *Ancient India*, Vol. 7, pp. 3-19.

Dales, G. F. (1966) : "Recent Trends in the Pre- and Proto-historic Archaeology in South India", *Proceedings of the American Philosophical Society*, Vol. 110 (2), pp. 130-139.

Godwin, H. (1956) : *The History of the British Flora*, Cambridge University Press.

Godwin, H. (1960) : "Radiocarbon Dating and Quaternary History in Britain", The Croonian Lecture, *Proceedings of the Royal Society*, B, Vol. 153, pp. 287-320.

Joshi, J. P. (1963) : *Comparative Stratigraphy of the Protohistoric Culture of the Indo-Pakistan Subcontinent*, (Lucknow).

Marshall, Sir John (1931) : *Mohenjo-daro and the Indus Civilization*, (London).

Post, L. von (1946) : "The Prospect of Pollen Analysis in the Study of the Earth's Climatic History", *New Phytologist*, Vol. 45, pp. 193-217.

Raikes, R. L. (1964) : "The end of the Ancient Cities of the Indus", *American Anthropologist*, Vol. 66 (2), pp. 284-299.

Raikes, R. L. (1965a) : "The Ancient Gabarbands of Baluchistan", *East and West*, Vol. 15 (1-2) pp. 3-12.

Raikes, R. L. (1965b) : "The Mohenjo-daro Floods", *Antiquity*, Vol. 39, pp. 155, 196-203.

Raikes, R. L., and Dyson, R. H. (1961) : "The Prehsitoric Climate of Baluchistan and the Indus Valley", *American Anthropologist*, Vol. 63 (2), pp 265-281.

Singh, G. (1963) : "A Preliminary Survey of the Post-glacial Vegetational History of the Kashmir Valley", *The Pelaeobotanist*, Vol. 12 (I), pp. 73-108.

Singh, G. (1967): "A Palynological Approach Towards the Resolution of some Important Desert Problems in Rajasthan" *Indian Geohydrology*, Vol. 3 (I), pp. 111-128.

Singh, G. (1970) : "History of Post-glacial Vegetation and Climate of the Rajasthan Desert" unpublished Report, submitted to the University of Wisconsin, Madison, U.S A.

Stein, Sir Aurel (1931) : "An Archaeological Tour in Gedrosia", *Memoirs of the Archaeological Survey of India*, Vol. 43.

Troup, R. S. (1921) : *The Silviculture of Indian Trees*, (Oxford).

Vats, M. S. (1940) : *Excavations at Harappa*, (Delhi).

Wheeler, Sir Mortimer (1968) : *The Cambridge History of India : The Indus Civilization*, 3rd Ed., Cambridge University Press.

* The original paper contains two figures and more details.